FINANCIAL INSTITUTIONS AND SERVICES

BANKS, SECURITIES AND THE VOLCKER RULE: BACKGROUND AND ISSUES

FINANCIAL INSTITUTIONS AND SERVICES

Additional books in this series can be found on Nova's website under the Series tab.

Additional E-books in this series can be found on Nova's website under the E-books tab.

BUSINESS ISSUES, COMPETITION AND ENTREPRENEURSHIP

Additional books in this series can be found on Nova's website under the Series tab.

Additional E-books in this series can be found on Nova's website under the E-books tab.

FINANCIAL INSTITUTIONS AND SERVICES

BANKS, SECURITIES AND THE VOLCKER RULE: BACKGROUND AND ISSUES

NICOLE A. GARCIA
EDITOR

Nova Science Publishers, Inc.
New York

For permission to use material from this book please contact us:
Telephone 631-231-7269; Fax 631-231-8175
Web Site: http://www.novapublishers.com

NOTICE TO THE READER

Additional color graphics may be available in the e-book version of this book.

LIBRARY OF CONGRESS CATALOGING-IN-PUBLICATION DATA
Banks, securities and the Volcker rule : background and issues / editor,
Nicole A. Garcia.
p. cm.
Contains reports previously published by Congressional Research Service.
Includes bibliographical references and index.
ISBN 978-1-61761-988-5 (hardcover)
1. Banking law--United States. 2. Bank investments--Law and
legislation--United States. I. Garcia, Nicole A. II. Carpenter, David
Hatcher. III. Murphy, M. Maureen.
KF968.6.B36 2010
346.73'082--dc22
2010041336

Published by Nova Science Publishers, Inc. † New York

CONTENTS

PREFACE

In 1933, during the first 100 days of President Franklin D. Roosevelt's New Deal, the Securities Act of 1933 and the Glass-Steagall Act (GSA) were enacted, setting up a pervasive regulatory scheme for the public offering of securities and generally prohibiting commercial banks from underwriting and dealing in those securities. Banks are subject to heavy, expensive prudential regulation, while the regulation of securities firms is predominantly built around registration, disclosure of risk, and the prevention and prosecution of insider trading and other forms of fraud. This book discusses the permissible proprietary trading activities of commercial banks and their subsidiaries under current law and then analyzes the Volcker Rule proposals under the House and Senate passed financial reform bills.

Chapter 1- In the wake of the recession of 2008, there have been calls to reexamine 1999's landmark financial services legislation, the Gramm-Leach-Bliley Act (GLBA; P.L. 106-102), which repealed certain provisions of the Banking Act of 1933, commonly referred to as the Glass-Steagall Act (GSA; 48 Stat. 162 §§ 16, 20, 21, and 32), which separated, to a certain degree, commercial banking (i.e., the activities engaged in by depository institutions with a bank charter, which this chapter generally will refer to as "banks" or "commercial banks") from investment banking (i.e., activities engaged in by securities firms).

Chapter 2- In 1933, during the first 100 days of President Franklin D. Roosevelt's New Deal, the Securities Act of 1933 and the Glass-Steagall Act (GSA) were enacted, setting up a pervasive regulatory scheme for the public offering of securities and generally prohibiting commercial banks from underwriting and dealing in those securities. Banks are subject to heavy, expensive prudential regulation, while the regulation of securities firms is predominately built around registration, disclosure of risk, and the prevention and prosecution of insider trading and other forms of fraud.

While there are two distinct regulatory systems, the distinguishing lines between the traditional activities engaged in by commercial and investment banks became increasingly difficult to discern as a result of competition, financial innovation, and technological advances in combination with permissive agency and judicial interpretation.

In: Banks, Securities and the Volcker Rule... ISBN: 978-1-61761-988-5
Editors: Nicole A. Garcia

Chapter 1

PERMISSIBLE SECURITIES ACTIVITIES OF COMMERCIAL BANKS UNDER THE GLASS-STEAGALL ACT (GSA) AND THE GRAMM-LEACH-BLILEY ACT (GLBA)

David H. Carpenter and M. Maureen Murphy

SUMMARY

In the wake of the recession of 2008, there have been calls to reexamine 1999's landmark financial services legislation, the Gramm-Leach-Bliley Act (GLBA; P.L. 106-102), which repealed certain provisions of the Banking Act of 1933, commonly referred to as the Glass-Steagall Act (GSA; 48 Stat. 162 §§ 16, 20, 21, and 32), which separated, to a certain degree, commercial banking (i.e., the activities engaged in by depository institutions with a bank charter, which this chapter generally will refer to as "banks" or "commercial banks") from investment banking (i.e., activities engaged in by securities firms).

This chapter explains the extent to which commercial banks, their subsidiaries, and affiliates were able to engage in securities activities, including securities underwriting, dealing, and brokerage, under the authorities of the GSA and other pre-GLBA banking laws, most notably the Bank Holding Company Act of 1956 (BHCA; 70 Stat. 133); how the volume and scope of these securities activities expanded over time, especially in the 1980s and 1990s; and how the GLBA changed the GSA construct by facilitating affiliations among commercial banks and securities firms, which paved the way for full-service financial companies like CitiGroup to offer deposit taking and full-scale securities dealing, securities underwriting, investment advising, and brokerage activities within a single holding company structure. To do this, the report first examines the historical differences between the regulatory structure of commercial and investment banks. It then provides a legal overview of the GSA's restrictions on securities activities and the evolution of how the federal agencies regulating commercial banks interpreted those restrictions over the course of approximately seven decades prior to enactment of the GLBA. The report then analyzes how the GLBA modified the GSA and the BHCA's securities restrictions and the resulting effect on the structure and activities of commercial banking companies.

The GLBA transformed the financial services regulatory system and structure by repealing certain provisions of the GSA and the BHCA and by establishing the financial holding company structure, which permits commercial banks and full-service investment banks (as well as insurance companies) to coexist under common control. However, GLBA's changes came after two decades of agency and judicial interpretations of the GSA and the BHCA, which significantly broadened the activities and presence of banks in the securities arena.

INTRODUCTION

In the wake of the recession of 2008, there have been calls to reexamine 1999's landmark financial services legislation, the Gramm-Leach-Bliley Act (GLBA),[1] which repealed certain provisions of the Banking Act of 1933, commonly referred to as the Glass-Steagall Act (GSA),[2] which imperfectly separated, to a certain degree, commercial banking (i.e., the activities engaged in by depository institutions with a bank charter,[3] which this chapter generally will refer to as "banks" or "commercial banks") from investment banking (i.e., activities engaged in by securities firms).

This chapter explains the extent to which commercial banks, their subsidiaries, and affiliates were able to engage in securities activities, including securities underwriting, dealing, and brokerage, under the authorities of the GSA and other pre-GLBA banking laws, most notably the Bank

Holding Company Act of 1956 (BHCA);[4] how the volume and scope of these securities activities expanded over time, especially in the 1980s and 1990s; and how the GLBA changed the GSA construct by facilitating affiliations among commercial banks and securities firms, which paved the way for full-service financial companies like CitiGroup to offer deposit taking and full-scale securities dealing, securities underwriting, investment advising, and brokerage activities within a single holding company structure. To do this, the report first examines the historical differences between the regulatory structure of commercial and investment banks. It then provides a legal overview of the GSA's restrictions on securities activities and the evolution of how the federal agencies regulating commercial banks interpreted those restrictions over the course of approximately seven decades prior to enactment of the GLBA. The report then analyzes how the GLBA modified the GSA and the BHCA's securities restrictions and the resulting effect on the structure and activities of commercial banking companies.

It should be noted that the GLBA addresses a wider range of issues beyond securities, such as insurance activities, that are not the focus of this chapter. This chapter also does not address the policy implications of amending the GLBA.

REGULATION OF COMMERCIAL BANKS AND SECURITIES FIRMS

In 1933, during the first one hundred days of President Franklin D. Roosevelt's New Deal, the Securities Act of 1933[5] and the GSA were enacted, setting up a pervasive regulatory scheme for the public offering of securities and generally prohibiting commercial banks from underwriting and dealing in those securities.[6] As a result, distinct regulatory systems developed in the United States for regulating banks, on the one hand, and securities firms on the other. As one commentator explains:

> Today, the principal financial regulations (and associated cost) that apply to a particular entity largely depend upon whether the entity is a bank, insurance company, or securities firm—definitions that, in many cases, were formed according to the business models that existed in the 1930s. ... Bank requirements have historically been more costly, reflecting the relative ability of securities firms and insurance companies to bear risk. Banks, however, were not disadvantaged so long as they only competed with other banks.[7]

As will be discussed in greater detail below, competition between banks[8] and securities firms began in earnest in the 1970s. The increased competition coupled with financial (e.g., securitization) and technological innovation (e.g., computers, automated teller machines (ATMs)) blurred the lines between the products, services, and activities offered by and engaged in commercial banks and securities firms (and insurance companies) even though their distinct regulatory systems largely remained the intact.[9]

Commercial banking is one of the most heavily regulated industries in the country. The federal bank regulators include the Office of the Comptroller of the Currency (OCC) for national banks; the Federal Reserve Board (FRB) for domestic operations of foreign banks and for state-chartered banks that are members of the Federal Reserve System (FRS); and the Federal Deposit Insurance Corporation (FDIC) for state-chartered banks and other state-chartered banking institutions that are not members of the FRS. The FDIC, which administers the Deposit Insurance Fund, also has regulatory power over state and national banks holding FDIC insured deposits. In general, companies owning or controlling at least one bank, called bank holding companies (BHCs),[10] are regulated on a consolidated basis by the FRB.[11] However, the FRB's authority as umbrella supervisor is subject to some important limitations, which are discussed in greater detail in the "Financial Holding Companies (FHCs): Expanded Activities for Bank Holding Companies" subsection of this chapter. (A few simple examples of bank and bank holding company structures can be found in **Appendix A** of this chapter.)

Prior to enactment of the National Bank Act of 1863 (NBA) ,[12] virtually all banks were chartered at the state level. The NBA established the national bank charter and, thus, this country's dual banking system, which persists today. Banks are institutions of limited power; they may only engage in the activities permissible pursuant to their charter, which generally limits them to the "business of banking" and all powers incidental to the business of banking.[13] In addition to these activity restrictions, banks are subject to capital standards, affiliation restrictions, management interlocking restrictions, and many other standards.[14] They also are subject to regular examinations to ensure they are being well-managed, conducting business in a safe and sound fashion, and complying with numerous consumer protection and other laws. All banks generally must be examined at least once every 18 months, but the largest banks have examiners on-site on a near constant basis.[15] Additionally, federal bank regulators have a full range of strong and flexible enforcement tools, such as prompt corrective action powers, to rectify any problems that are found during examinations.[16] Banks also are subject to a special resolution regime, called a conservatorship or receivership, to conserve, or more often, liquidate these institutions in an administrative, largely non-judicial, setting, which usually is administered by the FDIC and generally results in removal of the troubled-bank's existing management.[17]

One of the benefits of being a bank, and thus being subjected to heavy regulation, is access to what is referred to as the "federal safety net," (i.e., the FDIC's deposit insurance, the Federal Reserve's discount window lending facility,[18] and the Federal Reserve's payment system).

The regulation and oversight of securities firms is very different from that of banks. Securities firms may be primarily regulated by the Securities and Exchange Commission (SEC) at the federal level, or they may not be regulated directly at the federal level at all, which often is the case for hedge funds, private equity firms, and special purpose vehicles (SPVs).[19] Rather than regulating for safety and soundness, the SEC's regulatory regime is predominately built around registration, disclosure of risk, and the prevention and prosecution of insider trading and other forms of fraud. SEC-regulated firms generally are not subject to capital and liquidity standards or to regular safety and soundness examinations.[20] And aside from a general prohibition on accepting federally insured consumer deposits, securities firms generally are not subject to activity restrictions, as are banks.[21] As a result, these institutions generally do not have access to the federal safety net.[22]

From 2004 until September 2008, securities firms that did not have affiliations with a bank or thrift and that were organized in a holding company structure could have voluntarily agreed to consolidated regulation by the SEC as part of the now defunct Consolidated Supervised Entities program.[23] The GLBA provides a mechanism whereby a securities firm may voluntarily submit itself to umbrella SEC regulation on a consolidated basis by becoming an investment bank holding company, provided it is not affiliated with a bank or thrift.[24] Voluntary withdrawal from such supervision is also authorized.[25] SEC umbrella supervision of such companies apparently eliminated the need for the company to submit to European supervision. Until 2005, the European Union had no requirement for consolidated oversight of multinational financial services companies operating in Europe. That changed with the issuance of the European Financial Conglomerates Directive in December 2002, which requires such conglomerates to be subject to supervision at the holding company level as of 2005 or be subject to additional oversight by European authorities.[26] By the end of September 2008, most of the large investment bank holding companies that participated in the Consolidated Supervised Entities program either failed (e.g., Lehman Brothers), were acquired by a BHC (e.g.,

Bear Stearns, Merrill Lynch), or began a conversion to a financial holding company (FHC), a special type of BHC established by the GLBA (e.g., Goldman Sachs, Morgan Stanley).

THE GLASS-STEAGALL ACT

Overview of the GSA

There are four sections of the GSA that operate to restrict the securities activities of commercial banks. Section 16 (12 U.S.C. § 24(Seventh)) applies directly to national banks, and as a result of GSA § 5, indirectly to state member banks. [27] Although banks generally are precluded from underwriting and dealing in securities (particularly, equity securities), national banks have authority under GSA § 16 to deal in, underwrite, and purchase certain government (federal, state, and local) securities without quantitative limitation.[28] These types of securities are referred to as "bank eligible securities." All other securities are referred to as "bank ineligible securities." Section 16 does, however, generally allow banks to buy and sell securities on behalf of customers (e.g., making private placements of commercial paper and other securities with institutional investors).[29] Section 16 also provides banks with authority to make investment purchases of various *marketable* securities for their own accounts. Section 16 states that a bank may "purchase for its own account investment securities under such limitations and restrictions as the Comptroller of the Currency may prescribe."[30] Section 16 defines "investment securities" generally to mean debt securities, rather than equities.[31] OCC regulations exclude investments that are "speculative in nature" from this definition.[32] The regulations define "marketable" to include registered securities, municipal revenue bonds, investment grade securities sold in a Rule 144A offering,[33] and other securities "that can be sold with reasonable promptness at a price that corresponds reasonably to ... fair market value."[34] With the exception of obligations of the United States and other obligations backed by federal or state governments, the law imposes quantitative limits on the amount of securities which a national bank may hold for its own account.[35] Section 16 states in relevant part:

> The business of dealing in securities and stock by the association shall be limited to purchasing and selling such securities and stock without recourse, solely upon the order, and for the account of, customers, and in no

> case for its own account, and the association shall not underwrite any issue of securities or stock; Provided, That the association may purchase for its own account investment securities under such limitations and restrictions as the Comptroller of the Currency may by regulation prescribe. In no event shall the total amount of the investment securities of any one obligor or maker, held by the association for its own account, exceed at any time 10 per centum of its capital stock actually paid in and unimpaired and 10 per centum of its unimpaired surplus fund, except that this limitation shall not require any association to dispose of any securities lawfully held by it on August 23, 1935. As used in this section the term "investment securities" shall mean marketable obligations, evidencing indebtedness of any person, copartnership, association, or corporation in the form of bonds, notes and/or debentures commonly known as investment securities under such further definition of the term "investment securities" as may by regulation be prescribed by the Comptroller of the Currency. Except as hereinafter provided or otherwise permitted by law, nothing herein contained shall authorize the purchase by the association for its own account of any shares of stock of any corporation. The limitations and restrictions herein contained as to dealing in, underwriting and purchasing for its own account, investment securities shall not apply to obligations of the United States, or general obligations of any State or of any political subdivision thereof....

Section 20, which was repealed by the GLBA, applied to member banks (i.e., all national banks and all state-chartered banks that were members of the FRS). Section 20 prohibited member banks from affiliating with a business "engaged principally" in investment banking. This generally proscribed a bank from holding a majority ownership or controlling stake in a securities firm. Section 20 read:

> After one year from June 16, 1933, no member bank shall be affiliated in any manner described in subsection (b) of section 221a of this title [12][36] with any corporation, association, business trust, or other similar organization engaged principally in the issue, flotation, underwriting, public sale, or distribution at wholesale or retail or through syndicate participation of stocks, bonds, debentures, notes, or other securities: Provided, That nothing in this paragraph shall apply to any such organization which shall have been placed in formal liquidation and which shall transact no business except such as may be incidental to the liquidation of its affairs.

Section 21 (12 U.S.C. § 378) makes it illegal for any securities company to engage in deposit taking and preserves the authority of commercial banks to engage in the limited securities activities authorized under the GSA § 16 (12 U.S.C. § 24). Section 21 states, in relevant part:

> (a) After the expiration of one year after June 16, 1933, it shall be unlawful—
>
> (1) For any person, firm, corporation, association, business trust, or other similar organization, engaged in the business of issuing, underwriting, selling, or distributing, at wholesale or retail, or through syndicate participation, stocks, bonds, debentures, notes, or other securities, to engage at the same time to any extent whatever in the business of receiving deposits subject to check or to repayment upon presentation of a passbook, certificate of deposit, or other evidence of debt, or upon request of the depositor: Provided, That the provisions of this paragraph shall not prohibit national banks or State banks or trust companies (whether or not members of the Federal Reserve System) or other financial institutions or private bankers from dealing in, underwriting, purchasing, and selling investment securities, or issuing securities, to the extent permitted to national banking associations by the provisions of section 24 of this title: Provided further, That nothing in this paragraph shall be construed as affecting in any way such right as any bank, banking association, savings bank, trust company, or other banking institution, may otherwise possess to sell, without recourse or agreement to repurchase, obligations evidencing loans on real estate....

Finally, section 32 of the GSA, which was repealed by the GLBA, prohibited all member banks from having interlocking directorates and shared officers with companies "primarily engaged" in investment banking. This basically prevented employees, managers, and directors of commercial banks from also working for securities firms. It read:

> No officer, director, or employee of any corporation or unincorporated association, no partner or employee of any partnership, and no individual, primarily engaged in the issue, flotation, underwriting, public sale, or distribution, at wholesale or retail, or through syndicate participation, of stocks, bonds, or other similar securities, shall serve the same time as an officer, director, or employee of any member bank except in limited classes of cases in which the Board of Governors of the Federal Reserve System may allow such service by general regulations when in the judgment of the said Board it would not unduly influence the investment policies of such member bank or the advice it gives its customers regarding investments.

The BHCA expanded the scope of the GSA's affiliation restrictions by prohibiting companies owning or controlling banks (i.e., bank holding companies (BHCs)), from acquiring "ownership or control ... of any company which is not a bank or ... any company the activities of which had been determined by the ... [FRB] to be so closely related to banking as to be a proper incident thereto."[37]

As will be described in greater detail below, the expansion of permissible securities activities for BHCs and their subsidiaries derived largely from the FRB's interpretation of this provision of the BHCA and the "engaged principally" language of the GSA § 20, as well as, the OCC's interpretation of the "business of banking" under the GSA § 16.

Evolving Interpretation of the GSA and BHCA by the Agencies and the Courts

The OCC and the FRB are empowered to implement, enforce, and by extension, interpret (by regulation, guidance, or order) the subtleties and ambiguities of the GSA and the BHCA. For several decades after the enactment of the GSA, banks did not attempt to expand beyond traditional banking activities to a significant degree. This trend began to change in the 1970s. High inflation coupled with a consumer movement to interest-bearing accounts and investment products, such as money market funds offered by securities firms, reduced the profitability of traditional bank products.[38] Corporate consumers also began moving to securities firms for short-term lending (e.g., through the commercial paper market), which for some was less expensive than borrowing directly from banks. Facing lower profits and stiffer competition from securities firms, banks began seeking approval from regulators to engage in a greater universe of securities activities.[39] Additionally, regulators may have become less cautious as time passed after the Great Depression. One court explained in an opinion approving the OCC's interpretation of the GSA to allow bank subsidiaries to engage in discount brokerage activities:

> The early opinions of the Comptroller relied on by [the plaintiff] embody "an overcautious approach to bank regulation reflecting the atmosphere of the years immediately after the 1929 market crash ... ", and have gradually been disavowed by the Comptroller in the intervening decades. As the Comptroller stated in 1974, commenting on his reversal of an earlier decision disallowing

> bank charges for brokerage services: "This [earlier] view, like many others expressed by regulators, in the immediate post-depression decades, was designed to be ultra-conservative and to confine banks as narrowly as possible in their activities. However, in this regard, the office apparently went further in the direction of conservatism than did the Congress ...."[40]

Beginning in the 1970s and 1980s, requests for approval to engage in a greater universe of securities activities were largely granted by the OCC and the FRB and, in most cases, have been approved by courts. A seminal U.S. Supreme Court case involving agency interpretation of the GSA is *Investment Company Institute v. Camp.*[41] While ultimately holding against the OCC's specific interpretation of the GSA, the case is important because it paved the way for a broad reading of the act, as well as a policy of granting judicial deference to agency interpretation of the act.

Camp involved a challenge to the OCC's authority to authorize national banks to offer pooled investment funds that had much in common with open-end mutual funds. Ultimately, the Court found that GSA § 16 prohibited this type of activity, but it was the Court's method of analysis in reaching the holding that significantly impacted the banking world.

After an initial assessment that combining two traditional banking services—pooling trust funds and acting as a managing agent for bank customers—resulted in a close comparison with open-end mutual funds, the Court was reluctant to conclude that the Comptroller had violated the banking laws. It positioned itself to give deference to any reasonable interpretation of the GSA advanced by the Comptroller:

> It is settled that courts should give great weight to any reasonable construction of a regulatory statute adopted by the agency charged with the enforcement of that statute. The Comptroller of the Currency is charged with the enforcement of the banking laws to an extent that warrants the invocation of this principle with respect to his deliberative conclusions as to the meaning of these laws.[42]

In the case at hand, the Comptroller had merely issued regulations without alluding to the GSA, which the Court characterized as without "an administrative interpretation of §§ 16 and 21."[43]

Without an OCC interpretation to look to, the Court conducted its own exegesis of the GSA's legislative history to determine legislative intent. According to the Court:

> The Glass-Steagall Act reflected a determination that policies of competition, convenience, or expertise which might otherwise support the entry of commercial banks into the investment banking business were outweighed by the "hazards" and "financial dangers" that arise when commercial banks engage in the activities proscribed by the Act.[44]

The Court identified certain "promotional and other pressures" as "subtle hazards"[45] that had arisen before enactment of the GSA and that, according to the Court, Congress sought to eliminate through the 1933 legislation.[46] Among the subtle hazards explicitly named by the Court were: the association of a bank's reputation with its securities affiliate; the risk of offering the bank's credit line to customers of the securities affiliate; the reverberation on the bank's own business of securities losses suffered by bank depositors; and the conflict of interest between the bank's role as financial trustee and that of an investment broker who must promote certain securities.[47]

The Court concluded that the operation of an investment fund could involve the "subtle hazards" that the Congress sought to prevent through the GSA, such as the bank's reputation would be attached to the success of the fund; the bank may be pressured to rescue a failing fund; the bank may be tempted to extend credit, betray confidences, or give poor advice to customers for the sake of the fund; and the fund's activities could reflect poorly upon customer confidence in the bank.[48]

While in the short-term, the Court ruled against the OCC, the Court's opinion influenced subsequent decisional law by establishing a standard that deference would be paid to the OCC's reasoned conclusions that activities are authorized under the GSA and securities activities engaged in by banks that pass the "subtle hazards" test may be approved.[49]

The OCC and FRB began providing extensive legal reasoning in their orders and regulations approving securities activities of requesting banks. When these decisions were challenged as counter to the GSA or BHCA, courts looked to the reasonableness of the regulators' reasoning, rather than assessing whether that was the best interpretation or whether the court would have made the same decision. As a result, courts largely approved as valid interpretations of the banking laws the OCC's and FRB's decisions that expanded the securities activities deemed permissible for banks, BHCs, and their subsidiaries. Generally, agency approvals to expanded activities would be subject to certain conditions, such as that the activities be conducted in a safe and sound manner.

OCC Interpretations

Over the years, the OCC applied a number of different legal tests to determine whether an activity falls within the "business of banking."[50] These interpretations culminated in the 1995 U.S. Supreme Court decision, *NationsBank of North Carolina v. Variable Annuity Life Insurance Co. (VALIC)*, in which the Court stated:

> We expressly hold that the "business of banking" is not limited to the enumerated powers in § 24 Seventh and that the Comptroller therefore has discretion to authorize activities beyond those specifically enumerated. The exercise of the Comptroller's discretion, however, must be kept within reasonable bounds. Ventures distant from dealing in financial investments—for example, operating a general travel agency—may exceed those bounds.[51]

Subsequent to the *VALIC* decision, the OCC utilized the following test:

> Judicial cases affirming OCC interpretations establish that an activity is within the scope of this authority [12 U.S.C. § 24(Seventh)] if the activity: (1) is functionally equivalent to or a logical outgrowth of a traditional banking activity; (2) would respond to customer needs or otherwise benefit the bank or its customers; and (3) involve risks similar to those already assumed by banks.[52]

Pursuant to the GSA § 16, the OCC approved banks' and/or their operating subsidiaries' ability to become members of security exchanges[53] and commodity exchanges,[54] as well as to engage in discount brokerage;[55] investment company advising;[56] securities lending;[57] collective investment fund management (IRAs);[58] private placement of securities;[59] brokering and dealing in options and futures on foreign currency and other financial products;[60] general obligation municipal bond underwriting, dealing, and holding;[61] among others.

The OCC also has approved brokering and dealing in derivative contracts even where the bank is explicitly prohibited from directly investing in the asset underlying the contract, such as equity derivative swap contracts that are derived from equity securities.[62] This authority is explained in the Comptroller's Handbook:

> The OCC has recognized that national banks may enter into derivative transactions as principal when the bank may lawfully purchase and sell the underlying instrument or product for its own account, as a dealer or market-

> maker; or when the bank uses the transaction to hedge the risks arising from legally permissible activities.
>
> A national bank may also enter into derivative transactions as principal or agent when the bank is acting as a financial intermediary for its customers and whether or not the bank has the legal authority to purchase or sell the underlying instrument for its own account. Accordingly, a national bank may enter into derivative transactions based on commodities or equity securities, even though the bank may not purchase (or may be restricted in purchasing) the underlying commodity or equity security for its own account.[63]

Additionally, the OCC has approved banks' ability to buy and take physical possession of certain equity securities for the purpose of hedging customer-driven equity derivative transactions, subject to certain additional safeguards.[64]

FRB Interpretations

The FRB also approved similar activities for subsidiaries of BHCs and affiliates of member banks, through its interpretation of the BHCA. Until the 1980s, there had been no general FRB ruling establishing securities activities as an activity closely related to banking within the meaning of the BHCA. That changed with a series of FRB orders under the BHCA approving applications of BHCs to engage in investment banking activities through nonbank subsidiaries provided that the subsidiary was not "engaged principally" in the securities business. These subsidiaries became known as "section 20 subsidiaries."

To determine whether proposed securities activities were closely related to banking, the FRB generally employed a test articulated in *National Courier Association v. Board of Governors of the Federal Reserve System.*[65] This involved analyzing whether banks have generally provided the service, or functionally equivalent services, or services "so integrally related to the proposed activity as to require their provision in a separate form."[66] The FRB also indicated that these standards were not exclusive, that "the banking environment ... [was] changing," and that it would apply "any other factor that an applicant may advance to demonstrate a reasonable or close connection or relationship of the activity to banking or managing and controlling banks."[67] Although challenged by the securities industry, the FRB rulings were upheld by the courts.[68]

In these orders, the FRB approved BHC applications for wholly owned securities subsidiaries to deal in and underwrite both bank-eligible securities (i.e., the types of government securities which banks could underwrite and deal in under GSA § 16), and bank-ineligible securities (i.e., other types of securities in which member banks could invest but could not deal in or underwrite, provided the subsidiary was not "engaged principally" in the securities business within the meaning of GSA § 20). Under the rulings, for a securities subsidiary to be "engaged principally" in the securities business, its bank ineligible securities activities must exceed a certain percentage of gross revenue. Initially, the FRB set a 5%-10% limit on the amount of revenue from bank-ineligible securities in relation to the gross revenue of the company.[69] In regulations prescribed in 1996,[70] the FRB increased the gross revenue threshold limit to 25%.[71] Section 20 subsidiaries also were subject to oversight by the FRB and a number of "firewalls" designed to reduce conflicts between it and the bank affiliate and to enhance the bank's safety and soundness.[72] At the time of those regulations, the FRB had approved 41 section 20 subsidiaries to underwrite and deal bank-ineligible securities.[73]

By the time GLBA was enacted, the FRB had approved certain BHCs and their subsidiaries to underwrite and deal in the following bank ineligible securities: municipal bonds; commercial paper; mortgage-backed securities and other consumer-related securities; corporate debt securities; and corporate equity securities.[74] In addition to underwriting and dealing activities, the FRB also approved other securities activities such as the provision of investment advice;[75] the brokering of securities;[76] and others. The FRB promulgated the list of permissible nonbanking activities at 12 C.F.R. § 225.28(b).[77] (The entire regulation can be found at **Appendix B** of this chapter.) With respect to securities related activities, the regulation includes two distinct categories: (1) agency functions for customers and (2) transactions as principal (i.e., for the company's own account). In the latter category are the following: (1) "[u]nderwriting and dealing in government obligations and money market instruments"; (2) "[i]nvesting and trading activities"; and (3) "buying and selling bullion and related activities."

Landscape of the U.S. Financial Services Industry in the Run-Up to GLBA

By the mid-1990s, the market distinctions between commercial and investment banks had eroded tremendously but the disparate regulatory regimes, which was more costly for commercial banks than for securities firms, persisted. One banking scholar described the situation this way:

> History demonstrates that regulation of banks has not been based on any grand design. Rather, its foundations are built on a Civil War need for currency and a populist suspicion of concentrated wealth that peaked with the Great Depression. The result of this history was the creation of multiple state and federal regulators and the division of commercial and investment banking activities into separately regulated institutions. This New Deal regulatory scheme viewed commercial banking to be a single product that could be restricted to isolated institutions and intensively regulated "functionally." ...
>
> More importantly, modern banking no longer fits the 1930s profile around which financial services regulation is built. Banks are acting as conduits by generating loans that are securitized or syndicated and then sold rather than retained as assets in the manner of traditional commercial banking.[78]

As a result, there was a push for legislative changes to the regulation of commercial and investment banking. After about a decade of various levels of congressional interest in the matter,[79] the Gramm-Leach-Bliley Act of 1999 was enacted.

The Gramm-Leach-Bliley Act of 1999

Overview

Many of the federal and state restrictions on common control or ownership relationships (i.e., affiliations) between banks and securities firms ended with the 1999 enactment of the Gramm-Leach-Bliley Act (GLBA).[80] The GLBA repealed the GSA §§ 20 and 32.[81] It, thus, opened the way for what those sections had prohibited: affiliations between commercial banks and firms engaged principally in securities underwriting, and interlocking management and employee relationships between member banks and securities firms. The GLBA did not repeal the GSA §§ 16 and 21, which effectively prohibit banks from offering a full range of securities products and securities firms from taking deposits. The GLBA authorized securities activities in two types of bank affiliates—nonbank subsidiaries of holding companies and financial subsidiaries of banks.

GLBA also set forth conditions which must be satisfied before the expanded activities may occur and, in the case of bank subsidiaries, did not permit a full range of securities activities. The GLBA repealed the Bank Holding Company Act (BHCA)[82] provisions inhibiting affiliations among banking entities and insurance companies[83] and set up a mechanism by which companies owning banks may engage in insurance activities.[84]

Under the GLBA, expanded activities may be conducted in a form of BHC, known as a financial holding company (FHC), which may include full-scale securities and insurance subsidiaries as well as bank subsidiaries and the various kinds of nonbanking firms that had already been permitted within BHCs.[85] The GLBA did not repeal or modify section 16 of the GSA, thus national banks and state-chartered banks[86] continue to be prohibited from engaging in certain securities underwriting.[87] Under the GLBA, however, both national and state-chartered banks are authorized to form financial subsidiaries which may conduct a broad range of financial activities, including certain securities and insurance activities, without having to be part of a holding company structure. The same option is not accorded securities firms. The GLBA did not repeal the GSA § 21's prohibition on securities dealers "engaging in the business of receiving deposits."[88] Following the enactment of the GLBA, unless a securities firm had an affiliation with an insured depository institution as a result of approvals granted under previously existing laws, its only method of taking advantage of any synergy connected with sharing common ownership with a depository institution is through the FHC structure.[89] The GLBA did not require securities firms or insurance firms with pre-existing common control relationships with depository institutions outside of the BHC structure to convert to FHCs.[90] Thus, unitary thrift holding companies (i.e., savings and loan holding companies (S&LHCs) controlling only one savings association), may continue to engage in commercial and other non-conforming activities, including securities activities, provided the company is not sold and the savings association maintains a specified percentage of its assets invested in residential mortgages and, thereby, meets the qualified thrift lender test.[91]

Financial Holding Companies (FHCs): Expanded Activities for Bank Holding Companies

The GLBA introduced the financial holding company (FHC), a separate form of BHC for companies wishing to expand beyond the business of banking and closely related activities to a broader array of financial services. The GLBA permits FHCs to engage in and own companies engaging in (1) activities that are "financial in nature or incidental to such financial activity" or in (2) activities that are "complementary to a financial activity" and do "not pose a substantial risk to the safety and soundness of the depository."[92] The GLBA listed certain activities as "financial in nature,"[93] including all the nonbanking activities which had already been authorized for BHCs.[94] The GLBA empowered the FRB, in coordination with the Secretary of the Treasury, to issue orders or regulations supplementing that list.[95] (A full list of activities deemed financial in nature or incidental to financial activities pursuant to 12 U.S.C. § 1843(k)(4) and 12 C.F.R. § 228.86 can be found in this chapter's **Appendix C** and **Appendix D,** respectively.)

The GLBA established conditions which must be fulfilled before a BHC may become a FHC: all of the company's depository institution subsidiaries must be well managed and well capitalized, and the company must file a notice with the FRB of its intention to become a FHC, certifying that its depository institution subsidiaries meet those capital and management standards.[96]

Although the FRB retained its role as holding company regulator, the GLBA set up a regulatory framework for FHCs based on functional regulation that to some extent left gaps, particularly in the authority of the FRB over securities and insurance subsidiaries of FHCs. Under the GLBA, insured depository institutions, securities firms, insurance companies, and other financial services providers may coexist within one corporate structure with oversight responsibility dispersed among regulators based on the functions undertaken by each type of entity. Regulatory oversight of the various activities of the FHC is distributed as follows: (1) all of the federally chartered depository institution subsidiaries of the FHC are regulated by their chartering authority, either the OCC, the charterer of national banks, or the Office of Thrift Supervision (OTS), which charters federal savings associations of thrifts; (2) state-chartered depository subsidiaries are regulated by either the FRB or the FDIC, depending on whether or not they are members of the FRS; (3) all the securities subsidiaries of the FHC are regulated by the SEC or the appropriate state regulator; and (4) the insurance subsidiaries are subject to the functional regulation of state insurance authorities.[97] Insurance and securities activities conducted directly by banks are subject, to a certain extent, to SEC regulation. [98] Overall or umbrella supervision of the FHC or the BHC is the responsibility of the FRB.[99] To a great extent, particularly with respect to the nonbank subsidiaries of FHCs, the FRB's supervisory role is supplemental, rather than primary.[100] The GLBA also authorizes securities firms not affiliated with banks or thrifts to form investment bank holding companies voluntarily and, thereby, be supervised by the SEC, with the option of withdrawing from that arrangement.[101]

Although the GLBA authorizes the FRB to conduct examinations of the holding companies and subsidiaries, it imposes limitations on this authority in the case of functionally regulated subsidiaries.[102] As umbrella supervisor of a BHC or FHC, the FRB has greater authority over the holding company and any member bank subsidiary than it has over nonbank subsidiaries, such as securities companies, which are subject to functional regulation by the SEC. Examinations of nonbank subsidiaries may only be conducted on the basis of "reasonable cause."[103] Moreover, one section of federal law, enacted as part of the GLBA, places strict limits on the authority of the FRB to exercise prudential supervision, issue regulations, or bring enforcement actions against functionally regulated subsidiaries of FHCs, unless a separate statute provides the FRB explicit authority to bring an enforcement action.[104] Generally, this law requires the FRB to coordinate its supervision with that of the primary functional regulators. Although, the FRB has the authority to require securities subsidiaries of FHCs to submit reports on their financial condition and their efforts to comply with the GLBA or any law which the FRB has authority to enforce,[105] rather than imposing separate reporting requirements, the FRB must first make use of any reports that have been filed with the functional regulators.[106] The GLBA does not authorize the FRB to schedule routine periodic examinations of FHC subsidiaries that are functionally regulated by the SEC. The statute requires the FRB to defer to examinations made by the functional regulators, including the SEC.[107] If those examinations are not sufficient for its purposes, the FRB, in conducting examinations of a securities subsidiary of a FHC, must focus on the securities subsidiary's financial condition, the risks it poses to the safety and soundness of depository institution subsidiaries, and its compliance with laws that the FRB has authority to enforce, and its transactions with depository institution subsidiaries of the FHC.[108] Moreover, such examinations may only be conducted on the basis of "reasonable cause"[109] and must adhere to limits on their scope.[110] There also are prohibitions on the FRB's imposing capital standards on non-depository institution subsidiaries of the holding companies that are functionally regulated.[111] One provision states that an order of the FRB to a require a subsidiary of a BHC or a FHC to provide funds to a depository institution subsidiary is not enforceable against a functionally regulated insurance or securities company subsidiary if, in the case of a securities subsidiary, "the Securities and Exchange Commission ... determines in writing sent to the holding company and the ... [FRB] that the holding company shall not provide such funds or assets because such funds or assets would have a material adverse effect on the financial condition of the ...

broker, dealer, investment company, or investment adviser, as the case may be."[112] If the SEC refuses to permit the infusion of funds, the FRB is authorized to order the holding company to divest its depository subsidiary and, while divestiture is pending, to "impose any conditions or restrictions on the holding company's ownership or operation of the depository institution ... as are appropriate under the circumstances."[113]

As umbrella supervisor, the FRB's authority generally requires consultation with the functional regulators. There is at least one exception to this requirement. When the safety and soundness of a bank subsidiary of a FHC is threatened, the FRB has authority, without having to consult with the SEC, to proceed against a holding company. The law authorizes the FRB, upon "reasonable cause to believe that the continuation by a bank holding company of any activity or of ownership or control of any of its nonbank subsidiaries ... constitutes a serious risk to the financial safety, soundness, or stability of a bank holding company subsidiary bank and is inconsistent with sound banking practices," to terminate the activities of the nonbank subsidiary or the ownership of the holding company after providing notice and opportunity for a hearing.[114]

Financial Subsidiaries of Banks

Since the GLBA, not only may banks affiliate with securities firms within the FHC structure, national banks and state-chartered banks also may, subject to certain conditions, own or control financial subsidiaries that may engage in securities activities other than merchant banking (i.e., equity investment in private companies)[115] or insurance portfolio investing. Specifically, the GLBA authorized national banks to control or hold an interest in financial subsidiaries which could engage in "activities that are financial in nature or incidental to financial activity," as well as "activities that are permitted for national banks to engage in directly (subject to the same terms and conditions that govern the conduct of the activities by a national bank)."[116] It also provided authorization for state-chartered banks to control or hold interests in subsidiaries engaging "in activities as principal that would only be permissible for a national bank to conduct through a financial subsidiary."[117]

As is explained in greater detail in "The Glass-Steagall Act" section of this chapter, national banks have authority, under the GSA § 16, to deal in, underwrite and purchase certain government securities without quantitative limitation.[118] They also have authority to make private placements of securities.[119] Section 16 also provides national banks with authority to make investment purchases of various marketable securities for their own accounts. Section 16 states that a national bank may "purchase for its own account investment securities under such limitations and restrictions as the Comptroller of the Currency may prescribe."[120] Section 16 defines "investment securities" generally to mean debt securities, rather than equities.[121]

Financial subsidiaries, therefore, may also underwrite and deal in government securities, make private placements, and purchase debt securities. In addition, in general, financial subsidiaries may conduct any other activities authorized for FHCs with exceptions[122] for (1) underwriting insurance or annuities, except for certain grandfathered activities primarily related to credit insurance; (2) developing or investing in real estate; and (3) merchant banking[123] or insurance portfolio investing. There is also a provision permitting the Secretary of the Treasury to designate additional activities as financial in nature, in coordination with the FRB, based on the same standards as are applicable to the FRB when adding to the list of financial activities under the BHCA.[124]

For a national bank to hold a financial subsidiary that is engaging in financial activities as principal, rather than in an agency capacity, the bank and all of its depository institution affiliates must be well capitalized; there must be OCC approval; the bank must have a satisfactory rating under the Community Reinvestment Act;[125] the assets of all financial subsidiaries of the bank must not exceed the lesser of $50 billion or 45% of the assets of the bank; and for the largest banks, there are additional requirements.[126] State-chartered, federally insured banks have similar authority, provided that the bank and all of its insured depository institution affiliates are well capitalized and well managed.[127]

There are various provisions to insulate the bank from the activities of the financial subsidiary—assets and liabilities are not to be consolidated, and procedures must be implemented to maintain the separation between the bank and the subsidiary. If a national bank establishes a financial subsidiary, its procedures must cover the management of financial and operational risks to prevent the subsidiary's operations from infecting the bank and to insulate the bank from being held liable for actions of the subsidiary.[128] If the national bank, state-chartered bank, or any depository institution affiliate of the bank fails to maintain such procedures or falls below its requirements to be well-capitalized and well-managed, the OCC, the FRB, or the FDIC must act to secure compliance; until then, the appropriate federal banking agency may place limitations on the institution's conduct or activities. Additionally, the

OCC may require a national bank to divest control of the financial subsidiary if the conditions are not corrected within 180 days of receiving notice of noncompliance from the OCC.[129]

Federal Reserve Act Sections 23A and 23B Restrictions on Interaffiliate Transactions between Banks and Securities Subsidiaries of FHCs or Financial Subsidiaries of Banks

Current law provides federal regulators with certain tools to address the possibility that the health of depository institutions could be jeopardized by activities of affiliated companies. The GLBA authorizes the OCC and the FRB, within their respective jurisdictions, to impose restrictions, by regulation or order (i.e., having general applicability or limited to named institutions) on relationships or transactions between banks and their subsidiaries or between depository institution subsidiaries of a holding company and other affiliates of the holding company. These restrictions are predicated on, among other things, a finding that such restrictions are appropriate to prevent an evasion of the operative law or "to avoid a significant risk to the safety and soundness of depository institutions or any Federal deposit insurance fund or other adverse effects, such as undue concentration of resources, decreased or unfair competition, conflicts of interests, or unsound banking practices."[130] Sections 23A and 23B of the Federal Reserve Act (FRA) address the issue in a more comprehensive manner.[131] (The full statutory language of sections 23A and 23B is provided in **Appendix E** of this chapter.)

Sections 23A and 23B cover certain transactions involving a bank and its "affiliates" and define "affiliates" to include both holding company nonbank affiliates and financial subsidiaries of banks.[132] The transactions covered by sections 23A and 23B include extending credit to an affiliate; purchasing or investing in the securities of an affiliate; accepting the affiliate's securities as collateral for any extension of credit; and guaranteeing obligations of the affiliate.[133] The FRA section 23A[134] originally applied to member bank transactions with affiliates and has been extended to apply to all FDIC insured institutions.[135] It places an overall limit of 20% of a bank's capital and surplus on the amount of credit a bank may extend to affiliates[136] and a 10% limit on credit to any single affiliate, with exceptions to these percentages for financial subsidiaries of banks.[137] Section 23A also prohibits banks from purchasing "low quality assets" from an affiliate.[138]

The FRA § 23B,[139] which also applies to all insured banks,[140] has a general requirement that transactions with affiliates, including the transactions authorized under section 23A, be at arms length. This means that the statute requires that such transactions must be "on terms and under circumstances, including credit standards, that ... are at least as favorable to such bank ... as those prevailing at the time for comparable transactions with or involving other nonaffiliated companies, or ... in the absence of comparable transactions, on terms and under circumstances, including credit standards, that in good faith would be offered to, or would apply, to nonaffiliated companies." [141] Section 23B also imposes an arms length requirement on securities sales by a bank to an affiliate, including securities sales that are subject to repurchase agreements, and on other types of transactions including payment of money or services to an affiliate; transactions for which the affiliate is paid for its services to the bank; and, any transactions between the bank and a third party in which the affiliate participates or has a financial interest.[142] The statute provides the FRB with broad authority to "exempt transactions or relationships from the requirements of ... [section 23A] if it finds such exemptions to be in the public interest ...."[143]

The FRB has rulemaking authority[144] and has issued Regulation W[145] implementing sections 23A and 23B. Regulation W addresses the types of transactions between affiliates and member banks that are covered under sections 23A and 23B; the amounts which may be involved in such transactions; the safety and soundness requirements of such transactions; the collateral requirements for credit transactions with affiliates; the requirements for purchases of low-quality assets from affiliates; the standards by which transactions with other persons are treated as transactions with affiliates; the valuation principles to be employed for extensions of credit secured by affiliate securities; the rules for derivative transactions with affiliates; market terms requirements; coverage of asset purchase prohibitions; coverage of advertisement prohibitions; and purchases of the assets from one affiliate that relate to another affiliate. Also covered are collateral requirements of covered transactions[146] and specifications as to which transactions with third parties are to be treated as transactions with an affiliate.[147] There also are valuation and timing principles[148] and specific exemptions.[149] There is a procedure by which further exemptions may be requested and approved subject to a FRB finding that the exemption is "in the public interest and consistent with the purposes of section 23A."[150]

Under section 23B, banks are prohibited from entering into certain transactions with affiliates, including both their holding company affiliates and their financial subsidiaries. A bank may not purchase securities from an affiliate during the underwriting period if an affiliate of the bank is a principal underwriter of the securities, unless, prior to the initial public offering, the purchase has been approved by a majority of the bank's board of directors as a sound investment.[151] For a bank, acting as a fiduciary, to purchase securities from an affiliate, the purchase must have been authorized in the trust instrument, by court order, or under the laws of the jurisdiction governing the fiduciary relationship.[152] A bank may not advertise or enter into an agreement to take responsibility for the obligations of its affiliates or subsidiaries.[153]

Restrictions on Merchant Banking Investments and Investments in Private Equity Funds

Merchant Banking Investments. Under the GLBA[154] and rules promulgated jointly by the Secretary of the Treasury and the FRB,[155] FHCs with a securities affiliate or an insurance affiliate with an investment adviser affiliate[156] may engage in merchant banking activities (i.e., "directly or indirectly and as principal or on behalf of one or more persons, ... acquire or control any amount of shares, assets or ownership interests of a company or other entity that is engaged in any activity not otherwise authorized for the financial holding company")[157] under certain conditions. Such investments must be part of a bona fide underwriting or investment banking activity.[158] One of the conditions requires that the interests be held on a temporary basis[159] and, in general, no longer than ten years.[160] Another condition requires that the investment must be "part of a bona fide underwriting or merchant or investment banking activity."[161] Under the regulation, the shares in such investments may be acquired by any subsidiary of the FHC other than a depository institution subsidiary.[162] If assets other than debt or equity securities are involved, they must be "held or promptly transferred to a portfolio company."[163] "Portfolio company" is merely the term used for the company to which these assets must be transferred.[164] Depository institution subsidiaries of the FHC may not routinely manage the portfolio company.[165] There also are restrictions designed to prevent the FHC from routinely managing or operating the portfolio company.[166] For example, executive officers of the holding company and of certain subsidiaries of the holding company, including its securities broker and depository institution subsidiaries, may not serve as executive officers of the portfolio company.[167] Despite these restrictions, however, there is a provision which permits a FHC to routinely, but on a temporary basis,[168] manage a portfolio company; this may occur "only when intervention by the financial holding company is necessary or required to obtain a reasonable return on the financial holding company's investment in the portfolio company upon resale or other disposition of the investment, such as to avoid or address a significant operation loss or in connection with a loss of senior management at the portfolio company."[169] The FRB's prior approval is not generally required for a FHC to engage in merchant banking activities unless the proposed investment will result in the aggregate carrying value of all merchant banking investments to exceed a certain level.[170]

Merchant Banking Investments Through a Private Equity Fund. A FHC also may make merchant banking investments though a private equity fund that makes investments in nonfinancial companies, provided the private equity fund meets certain qualifications and the FHC's investments comply with requirements for merchant banking. "Private equity fund" is defined, for this purpose, as a company "formed for the purpose of and exclusively engaged in the business of investing in shares, assets, and ownership interests of financial and nonfinancial companies for resale or other disposition."[171] The private equity company must not be an operating company; no more than 25% of its equity may be held by the FHC or any of its officers, directors, employees or principal shareholders; its term must be no longer than 15 years; and it must not have been formed to evade the merchant banking restrictions on FHCs.[172] If a FHC makes investments through a private equity fund, the investments will generally be subject to a 15-year limitation rather than 10 years as would be the case were the FHC to make direct investments.[173] If a FHC controls a private equity fund, the FHC may not routinely operate the private equity fund.[174]

FRA §§ 23A and 23B apply to transactions between the FHC and its subsidiaries and the private equity fund only if control exists. The regulations presume control, for applicability of sections 23A and 23B, if the FHC controls more than 15 percent of the private equity firm's total equity.[175] This presumption may be rebutted with contrary evidence presented to the FRB or by showing the existence of any one of the following presumptions against control: (1) none of the FHC's officers, directors, or employees serves as directors or trustees of the firm; (2) another person or entity holds more of the total equity of the firm than does the FHC and no more than one of the FHC's officers, directors, or employees serve as directors or trustees of the firm; (3) another person or entity controls more than 50 percent of the voting shares of the firm and the officers, directors, or employees of the FHC do not constitute a majority of the directors or trustees of the firm.[176]

On June 22, 2000, the FRB issued guidance for FHCs on equity investment and merchant banking.[177] This guidance focuses on sound policies and practices, including board of directors oversight; limits on and controls with respect to types and amounts of investments; periodic reviews of investments and of the component elements of the investment process; assessment of possible investment performance under various circumstances; internal controls adopted to types of investments; exit strategies; and capital allocation based on risk. There are also guidelines on transactions involving the portfolio company which are not subject to the FRA §§ 23A and 23B.[178] FHCs are urged to "have systems and policies in place to monitor transactions between the holding company, or a non-depository institution subsidiary of the holding company, and a portfolio company ... [to] assure that the risks of these transactions, including exposures of the holding company on a consolidated basis to a single portfolio company, are reasonably limited and that all transactions are on reasonable terms, with special attention paid to transactions that are not on market terms."[179]

CONCLUSION

The Glass-Steagall Act of 1933 imposed regulatory barriers between commercial banks and investment banks, which were further buttressed by provisions of the Bank Holding Company Act of 1956. However, those barriers were not impermeable. Through competition, financial innovation, and technological advances, the distinguishing lines between the traditional activities engaged in by commercial and investment banks became increasingly difficult to discern. The Federal Reserve Board and the Office of the Comptroller of the Currency issued a series of broadly applicable regulations and individually applicable orders, liberally interpreting limitations of the Glass-Steagall Act and the Bank Holding Company Act, which generally met judicial approval. The result was the incremental expansion of the types and levels of securities activities permissible for bank holding companies and financial subsidiaries of banks. The Gramm-Leach-Bliley Act of 1999 continued this trend by repealing certain provisions of the GSA and the BHCA and by establishing the financial holding company structure, which permits commercial banks and full-service investment banks (as well as insurance companies) to coexist under common control. However, as much as GLBA transformed the financial services regulatory system and structure, those changes came after two decades of agency and judicial interpretations of the Glass-Steagall Act and the Bank Holding Company Act, which significantly broadened the activities and presence of banks in the securities arena.

APPENDIX A. FORMS OF BANKING ORGANIZATIONS

The structure of banks can be complex. Currently, the regulator of a particular activity of a bank or its subsidiary in part depends on the activity of the subsidiary or its charter, as described above. The following flow charts provide simplified representations of various bank structures. In some cases, the umbrella bank and its subsidiaries may have different regulators.

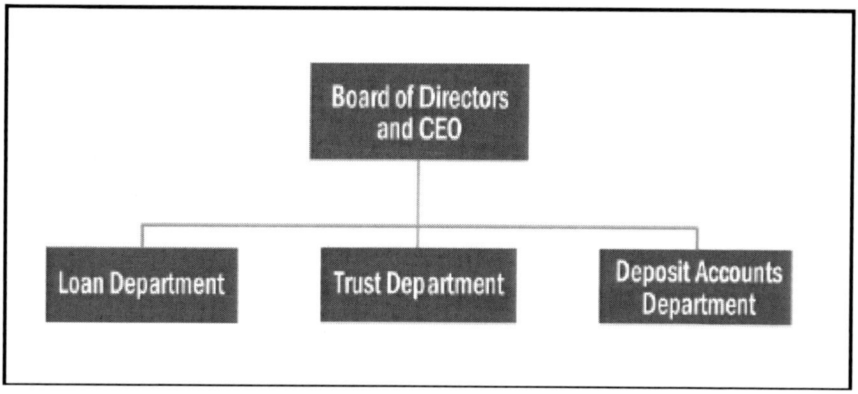

Figure A-1. National Bank.

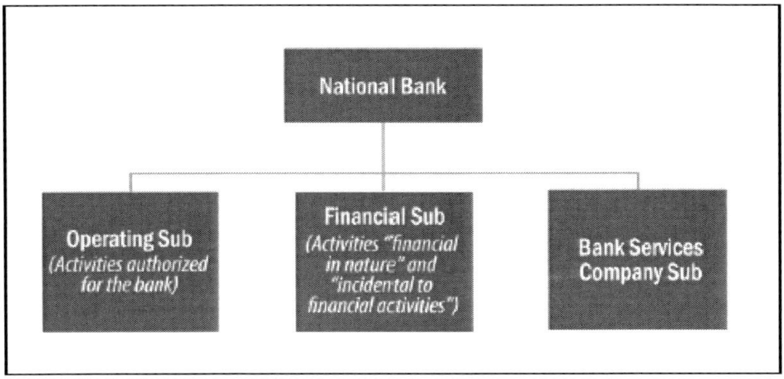

Figure A-2. National Bank and Subsidiaries (Sub).

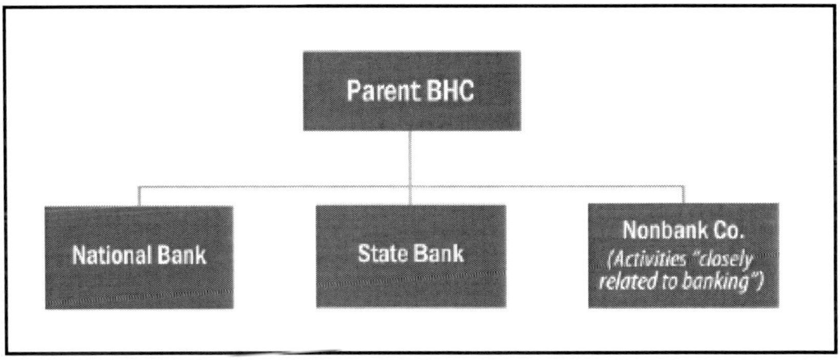

Figure A-3. Bank Holding Company.

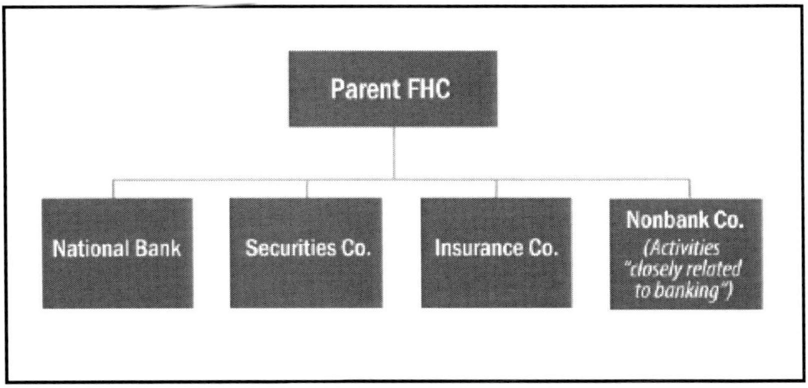

Figure A-4. Financial Holding Company.

APPENDIX B. PERMISSIBLE NONBANKING ACTIVITIES: 12 C.F.R. § 225.28

List of Permissible Nonbanking Activities

(a) *Closely related nonbanking activities.* The activities listed in paragraph (b) of this section are so closely related to banking or managing or controlling banks as to be a proper incident thereto, and may be engaged in by a bank holding company or its subsidiary in accordance with the requirements of this regulation.

(b) *Activities determined by regulation to be permissible—*

(1) *Extending credit and servicing loans.* Making, acquiring, brokering, or servicing loans or other extensions of credit (including factoring, issuing letters of credit and accepting drafts) for the company's account or for the account of others.

(2) *Activities related to extending credit.* Any activity usual in connection with making, acquiring, brokering or servicing loans or other extensions of credit, as determined by the Board. The Board has determined that the following activities are usual in connection with making, acquiring, brokering or servicing loans or other extensions of credit:

(i) *Real estate and personal property appraising.* Performing appraisals of real estate and tangible and intangible personal property, including securities.

(ii) *Arranging commercial real estate equity financing.* Acting as intermediary for the financing of commercial or industrial income-producing real estate by arranging for the transfer of the title, control, and risk of such a real estate project to one or more investors, if the bank holding company and its affiliates do not have an interest in, or participate in managing or developing, a real estate project for which it arranges equity financing, and do not promote or sponsor the development of the property.

(iii) *Check-guaranty services.* Authorizing a subscribing merchant to accept personal checks tendered by the merchant's customers in payment for goods and services, and purchasing from the merchant validly authorized checks that are subsequently dishonored.

(iv) *Collection agency services.* Collecting overdue accounts receivable, either retail or commercial.

(v) *Credit bureau services.* Maintaining information related to the credit history of consumers and providing the information to a credit grantor who is considering a borrower's application for credit or who has extended credit to the borrower.

(vi) *Asset management, servicing, and collection activities.* Engaging under contract with a third party in asset management, servicing, and collection[180] of assets of a type that an insured depository institution may originate and own, if the company does not engage in real property management or real estate brokerage services as part of these services.

(vii) *Acquiring debt in default.* Acquiring debt that is in default at the time of acquisition, if the company:

(A) Divests shares or assets securing debt in default that are not permissible investments for bank holding companies, within the time period required for divestiture of property acquired in satisfaction of a debt previously contracted under §225.12(b);[181]

(B) Stands only in the position of a creditor and does not purchase equity of obligors of debt in default (other than equity that may be collateral for such debt); and

(C) Does not acquire debt in default secured by shares of a bank or bank holding company.

(viii) *Real estate settlement servicing.* Providing real estate settlement services.[182]

(3) *Leasing personal or real property.* Leasing personal or real property or acting as agent, broker, or adviser in leasing such property if:

(i) The lease is on a nonoperating basis;[183]

(ii) The initial term of the lease is at least 90 days;

(iii) In the case of leases involving real property:

(A) At the inception of the initial lease, the effect of the transaction will yield a return that will compensate the lessor for not less than the lessor's full investment in the property plus the estimated total cost of financing the property over the term of the lease from rental payments, estimated tax benefits, and the estimated residual value of the property at the expiration of the initial lease; and

(B) The estimated residual value of property for purposes of paragraph (b)(3)(iii)(A) of this section shall not exceed 25 percent of the acquisition cost of the property to the lessor.

(4) Operating nonbank depository institutions—

(i) *Industrial banking.* Owning, controlling, or operating an industrial bank, Morris Plan bank, or industrial loan company, so long as the institution is not a bank.

(ii) *Operating savings association.* Owning, controlling, or operating a savings association, if the savings association engages only in deposit-taking activities, lending, and other activities that are permissible for bank holding companies under this subpart C.

(5) *Trust company functions.* Performing functions or activities that may be performed by a trust company (including activities of a fiduciary, agency, or custodial nature), in the manner authorized by federal or state law, so long as the company is not a bank for purposes of section 2(c) of the Bank Holding Company Act.

(6) *Financial and investment advisory activities.* Acting as investment or financial advisor to any person, including (without, in any way, limiting the foregoing):

(i) Serving as investment adviser (as defined in section 2(a)(20) of the Investment Company Act of 1940, 15 U.S.C. 80a–2(a)(20)), to an investment company registered under that act, including sponsoring, organizing, and managing a closed-end investment company;

(ii) Furnishing general economic information and advice, general economic statistical forecasting services, and industry studies;

(iii) Providing advice in connection with mergers, acquisitions, divestitures, investments, joint ventures, leveraged buyouts, recapitalizations, capital structurings, financing transactions and similar transactions, and conducting financial feasibility studies;[184]

(iv) Providing information, statistical forecasting, and advice with respect to any transaction in foreign exchange, swaps, and similar transactions, commodities, and any forward contract, option, future, option on a future, and similar instruments;

(v) Providing educational courses, and instructional materials to consumers on individual financial management matters; and

(vi) Providing tax-planning and tax-preparation services to any person.

(7) Agency transactional services for customer investments—

(i) *Securities brokerage.* Providing securities brokerage services (including securities clearing and/or securities execution services on an exchange), whether alone or in combination with investment advisory services, and incidental activities (including related securities credit activities and custodial services), if the securities brokerage services are restricted to buying and selling securities solely as agent for the account of customers and do not include securities underwriting or dealing.

(ii) *Riskless principal transactions.* Buying and selling in the secondary market all types of securities on the order of customers as a "riskless principal" to the extent of engaging in a transaction in which the company, after receiving an order to buy (or sell) a security from a customer, purchases (or sells) the security for its own account to offset a contemporaneous sale to (or purchase from) the customer. This does not include:

(A) Selling bank-ineligible securities[185] at the order of a customer that is the issuer of the securities, or selling bank-ineligible securities in any transaction where the company has a contractual agreement to place the securities as agent of the issuer; or

(B) Acting as a riskless principal in any transaction involving a bank-ineligible security for which the company or any of its affiliates acts as underwriter (during the period of the underwriting or for 30 days thereafter) or dealer.[186]

(iii) *Private placement services.* Acting as agent for the private placement of securities in accordance with the requirements of the Securities Act of 1933 (1933 Act) and the rules of the Securities and Exchange Commission, if the company engaged in the activity does not purchase or repurchase for its own account the securities being placed, or hold in inventory unsold portions of issues of these securities.

(iv) *Futures commission merchant.* Acting as a futures commission merchant (FCM) for unaffiliated persons in the execution, clearance, or execution and clearance of any futures contract and option on a futures contract traded on an exchange in the United States or abroad if:

(A) The activity is conducted through a separately incorporated subsidiary of the bank holding company, which may engage in activities other than FCM activities (including, but not limited to, permissible advisory and trading activities); and

(B) The parent bank holding company does not provide a guarantee or otherwise become liable to the exchange or clearing association other than for those trades conducted by the subsidiary for its own account or for the account of any affiliate.

(v) *Other transactional services.* Providing to customers as agent transactional services with respect to swaps and similar transactions, any transaction described in paragraph (b)(8) of this section, any transaction that is permissible for a state member bank, and any other transaction involving a forward contract, option, futures, option on a futures or similar contract (whether traded on an exchange or not) relating to a commodity that is traded on an exchange.

(8) *Investment transactions as principal—*

(i) *Underwriting and dealing in government obligations and money market instruments.* Underwriting and dealing in obligations of the United States, general obligations of states and their political subdivisions, and other obligations that state member banks of the Federal Reserve System may be authorized to underwrite and deal in under 12 U.S.C. 24 and 335, including banker's acceptances and certificates of deposit, under the same limitations as would be applicable if the activity were performed by the bank holding company's subsidiary member banks or its subsidiary nonmember banks as if they were member banks.

(ii) *Investing and trading activities.* Engaging as principal in:

(A) Foreign exchange;

(B) Forward contracts, options, futures, options on futures, swaps, and similar contracts, whether traded on exchanges or not, based on any rate, price, financial asset (including gold, silver, platinum, palladium, copper, or any other metal approved by the Board), nonfinancial asset, or group of assets, other than a bank-ineligible security,[187] if:

(*1*) A state member bank is authorized to invest in the asset underlying the contract;

(*2*) The contract requires cash settlement;

(*3*) The contract allows for assignment, termination, or offset prior to delivery or expiration, and the company—

(*i*) Makes every reasonable effort to avoid taking or making delivery of the asset underlying the contract; or

(*ii*) Receives and instantaneously transfers title to the underlying asset, by operation of contract and without taking or making physical delivery of the asset; or

(*4*) The contract does not allow for assignment, termination, or offset prior to delivery or expiration and is based on an asset for which futures contracts or options on futures contracts have been approved for trading on a U.S. contract market by the Commodity Futures Trading Commission, and the company—

(*i*) Makes every reasonable effort to avoid taking or making delivery of the asset underlying the contract; or

(*ii*) Receives and instantaneously transfers title to the underlying asset, by operation of contract and without taking or making physical delivery of the asset.

(C) Forward contracts, options,[188] futures, options on futures, swaps, and similar contracts, whether traded on exchanges or not, based on an index of a rate, a price, or the value of any financial asset, nonfinancial asset, or group of assets, if the contract requires cash settlement.

(iii) *Buying and selling bullion, and related activities.* Buying, selling and storing bars, rounds, bullion, and coins of gold, silver, platinum, palladium, copper, and any other metal approved by the Board, for the company's own account and the account of others, and providing incidental services such as arranging for storage, safe custody, assaying, and shipment.

(9) Management consulting and counseling activities—

(i) Management consulting.

(A) Providing management consulting advice:[189]

(*1*) On any matter to unaffiliated depository institutions, including commercial banks, savings and loan associations, savings banks, credit unions, industrial banks, Morris Plan banks, cooperative banks, industrial loan companies, trust companies, and branches or agencies of foreign banks;

(*2*) On any financial, economic, accounting, or audit matter to any other company.

(B) A company conducting management consulting activities under this subparagraph and any affiliate of such company may not:

(*1*) Own or control, directly or indirectly, more than 5 percent of the voting securities of the client institution; and

(*2*) Allow a management official, as defined in 12 CFR 212.2(h), of the company or any of its affiliates to serve as a management official of the client institution, except where such interlocking relationship is permitted pursuant to an exemption granted under 12 CFR 212.4(b) or otherwise permitted by the Board.

(C) A company conducting management consulting activities may provide management consulting services to customers not described in paragraph (b)(9)(i)(A)(*1*) of this section or regarding matters not described in paragraph (b)(9)(i)(A)(*2*) of this section, if the total annual revenue derived from those management consulting services does not exceed 30 percent of the company's total annual revenue derived from management consulting activities.

(ii) *Employee benefits consulting services.* Providing consulting services to employee benefit, compensation and insurance plans, including designing plans, assisting in the implementation of plans, providing administrative services to plans, and developing employee communication programs for plans.

(iii) *Career counseling services.* Providing career counseling services to:

(A) A financial organization[190] and individuals currently employed by, or recently displaced from, a financial organization;

(B) Individuals who are seeking employment at a financial organization; and

(C) Individuals who are currently employed in or who seek positions in the finance, accounting, and audit departments of any company.

(10) *Support services—*

(i) *Courier services.* Providing courier services for:

(A) Checks, commercial papers, documents, and written instruments (excluding currency or bearer-type negotiable instruments) that are exchanged among banks and financial institutions; and

(B) Audit and accounting media of a banking or financial nature and other business records and documents used in processing such media.[191]

(ii) *Printing and selling MICR-encoded items.* Printing and selling checks and related documents, including corporate image checks, cash tickets, voucher checks, deposit slips, savings withdrawal packages, and other forms that require Magnetic Ink Character Recognition (MICR) encoding.

(11) *Insurance agency and underwriting—*

(i) *Credit insurance.* Acting as principal, agent, or broker for insurance (including home mortgage redemption insurance) that is:

(A) Directly related to an extension of credit by the bank holding company or any of its subsidiaries; and

(B) Limited to ensuring the repayment of the outstanding balance due on the extension of credit[192] in the event of the death, disability, or involuntary unemployment of the debtor.

(ii) *Finance company subsidiary.* Acting as agent or broker for insurance directly related to an extension of credit by a finance company[193] that is a subsidiary of a bank holding company, if:

(A) The insurance is limited to ensuring repayment of the outstanding balance on such extension of credit in the event of loss or damage to any property used as collateral for the extension of credit; and

(B) The extension of credit is not more than $10,000, or $25,000 if it is to finance the purchase of a residential manufactured home[194] and the credit is secured by the home; and

(C) The applicant commits to notify borrowers in writing that:

(*1*) They are not required to purchase such insurance from the applicant;

(*2*) Such insurance does not insure any interest of the borrower in the collateral; and

(*3*) The applicant will accept more comprehensive property insurance in place of such single-interest insurance.

(iii) *Insurance in small towns.* Engaging in any insurance agency activity in a place where the bank holding company or a subsidiary of the bank holding company has a lending office and that:

(A) Has a population not exceeding 5,000 (as shown in the preceding decennial census); or

(B) Has inadequate insurance agency facilities, as determined by the Board, after notice and opportunity for hearing.

(iv) *Insurance-agency activities conducted on May 1, 1982.* Engaging in any specific insurance-agency activity[195] if the bank holding company, or subsidiary conducting the specific activity, conducted such activity on May 1, 1982, or received Board approval to conduct such activity on or before May 1, 1982.[196] A bank holding company or subsidiary engaging in a specific insurance agency activity under this clause may:

(A) Engage in such specific insurance agency activity only at locations:

(*1*) In the state in which the bank holding company has its principal place of business (as defined in 12 U.S.C. 1842(d));

(*2*) In any state or states immediately adjacent to such state; and

(*3*) In any state in which the specific insurance-agency activity was conducted (or was approved to be conducted) by such bank holding company or subsidiary thereof or by any other subsidiary of such bank holding company on May 1, 1982; and

(B) Provide other insurance coverages that may become available after May 1, 1982, so long as those coverages insure against the types of risks as (or are otherwise functionally equivalent to) coverages sold or approved to be sold on May 1, 1982, by the bank holding company or subsidiary.

(v) *Supervision of retail insurance agents.* Supervising on behalf of insurance underwriters the activities of retail insurance agents who sell:

(A) Fidelity insurance and property and casualty insurance on the real and personal property used in the operations of the bank holding company or its subsidiaries; and

(B) Group insurance that protects the employees of the bank holding company or its subsidiaries.

(vi) *Small bank holding companies.* Engaging in any insurance-agency activity if the bank holding company has total consolidated assets of $50 million or less. A bank holding company performing insurance-agency activities under this paragraph may not engage in the sale of life insurance or annuities except as provided in paragraphs (b)(11) (i) and (iii) of this section, and it may not continue to engage in insurance-agency activities pursuant to this provision more than 90 days after the end of the quarterly reporting period in which total assets of the holding company and its subsidiaries exceed $50 million.

(vii) *Insurance-agency activities conducted before 1971.* Engaging in any insurance-agency activity performed at any location in the United States directly or indirectly by a bank holding company that was engaged in insurance-agency activities prior to January 1, 1971, as a consequence of approval by the Board prior to January 1, 1971.

(12) *Community development activities—*

(i) *Financing and investment activities.* Making equity and debt investments in corporations or projects designed primarily to promote community welfare, such as the economic rehabilitation and development of low-income areas by providing housing, services, or jobs for residents.

(ii) *Advisory activities.* Providing advisory and related services for programs designed primarily to promote community welfare.

(13) *Money orders, savings bonds, and traveler's checks.* The issuance and sale at retail of money orders and similar consumer-type payment instruments; the sale of U.S. savings bonds; and the issuance and sale of traveler's checks.

(14) *Data processing.*

(i) Providing data processing, data storage and data transmission services, facilities (including data processing, data storage and data transmission hardware, software, documentation, or operating personnel), databases, advice, and access to such services, facilities, or data-bases by any technological means, if:

(A) The data to be processed, stored or furnished are financial, banking or economic; and

(B) The hardware provided in connection therewith is offered only in conjunction with software designed and marketed for the processing, storage and transmission of financial, banking, or economic data, and where the general purpose hardware does not constitute more than 30 percent of the cost of any packaged offering.

(ii) A company conducting data processing, data storage, and data transmission activities may conduct data processing, data storage, and data transmission activities not described in paragraph (b)(14)(i) of this section if the total annual revenue derived from those activities does not exceed 49 percent of the company's total annual revenues derived from data processing, data storage and data transmission activities.

Appendix C. Activities Considered Financial in Nature under Section 4(k)(4) of the Bank Holding Company Act, 12 U.S. § 1843(k)(4)

Activities That Are Financial in Nature

For purposes of this subsection, the following activities shall be considered to be financial in nature:

(A) Lending, exchanging, transferring, investing for others, or safeguarding money or securities.

(B) Insuring, guaranteeing, or indemnifying against loss, harm, damage, illness, disability, or death, or providing and issuing annuities, and acting as principal, agent, or broker for purposes of the foregoing, in any State.

(C) Providing financial, investment, or economic advisory services, including advising an investment company (as defined in section 3 of the Investment Company Act of 1940).

(D) Issuing or selling instruments representing interests in pools of assets permissible for a bank to hold directly.

(E) Underwriting, dealing in, or making a market in securities.

(F) Engaging in any activity that the Board has determined, by order or regulation that is in effect on the date of the enactment of the Gramm-Leach-Bliley Act, to be so closely related to banking or managing or controlling banks as to be a proper incident thereto (subject to the same terms and conditions contained in such order or regulation, unless modified by the Board).

(G) Engaging, in the United States, in any activity that—

(i) a bank holding company may engage in outside the United States; and

(ii) the Board has determined, under regulations prescribed or interpretation issued pursuant to subsection (c)(13) (as in effect on the day before the date of the enactment of the Gramm-Leach-Bliley Act) to be usual in connection with the transaction of banking or other financial operations abroad.

(H) Directly or indirectly acquiring or controlling, whether as principal, on behalf of 1 or more entities (including entities, other than a depository institution or subsidiary of a depository institution, that the bank holding company controls), or otherwise, shares, assets, or ownership interests (including debt or equity securities, partnership interests, trust certificates, or other instruments representing ownership) of a company or other entity, whether or not constituting control of such company or entity, engaged in any activity not authorized pursuant to this section if—

(i) the shares, assets, or ownership interests are not acquired or held by a depository institution or subsidiary of a depository institution;

(ii) such shares, assets, or ownership interests are acquired and held by—

(I) a securities affiliate or an affiliate thereof; or

(II) an affiliate of an insurance company described in subparagraph (I)(ii) that provides investment advice to an insurance company and is registered pursuant to the Investment Advisors Act of 1940, or an affiliate of such investment advisor; as part of a bona fide underwriting or merchant or investment banking activity, including investment activities engaged in for the purpose of appreciation and ultimate resale or disposition of the investment;

(iii) such shares, assets, or ownership interests are held for a period of time to enable the sale or disposition thereof on a reasonable basis consistent with the financial viability of the activities described in clause (ii); and

(iv) during the period such shares, assets or ownership interests are held, the bank holding company does not routinely manage or operate such company or entity except as may be necessary or required to obtain a reasonable return on investment upon resale or disposition.

(I) Directly or indirectly acquiring or controlling, whether as principal, on behalf of 1 or more entities (including entities, other than a depository institution or subsidiary of a depository institution, that the bank holding company controls) or otherwise, shares, assets, or ownership interests, trust certificates or other instruments representing ownership) of a company or other entity, whether or not constituting control of such company or entity, engaged in any activity not authorized pursuant to this section if—

(i) the shares, assets, or ownership interests are not acquired or held by a depository institution or a subsidiary of a depository institution;
(ii) such shares, assets, or ownership interests are acquired and held by an insurance company that is predominantly engaged in underwriting life, accident and health, or property and casualty insurance (other that credit-related insurance) or providing and issuing annuities;
(iii) such shares, assets, or ownership interests represent an investment made in the ordinary course of business of such insurance company in accordance with relevant State law governing such investment; and
(iv) during the period such shares, assets, or ownership interests are held, the bank holding company does not routinely manage or operate such company except as may be necessary or required to obtain a reasonable return on investment.

[Footnotes omitted.]

APPENDIX D. ACTIVITIES PERMISSIBLE FOR FINANCIAL HOLDING COMPANIES UNDER 12 C.F.R. § 225.86

Activities That Are Financial in Nature or Incidental to a Financial Activity

(a) Activities determined to be closely related to banking.
(1) Any activity that the Board had determined by regulation prior to November 12, 1999, to be so closely related to banking as to be a proper incident thereto, subject to the terms and conditions contained in this part, unless modified by the Board. These activities are listed in §225.28.
(2) Any activity that the Board had determined by an order that was in effect on November 12, 1999, to be so closely related to banking as to be a proper incident thereto, subject to the terms and conditions contained in this part and those in the authorizing orders. These activities are:
(i) Providing administrative and other services to mutual funds (*Societe Generale,* 84 Federal Reserve Bulletin 680 (1998));

(ii) Owning shares of a securities exchange (*J.P. Morgan & Co, Inc., and UBS AG,* 86 Federal Reserve Bulletin 61 (2000));

(iii) Acting as a certification authority for digital signatures and authenticating the identity of persons conducting financial and nonfinancial transactions (*Bayerische Hypo- und Vereinsbank AG, et al.,* 86 Federal Reserve Bulletin 56 (2000));

(iv) Providing employment histories to third parties for use in making credit decisions and to depository institutions and their affiliates for use in the ordinary course of business (*Norwest Corporation,* 81 Federal Reserve Bulletin 732 (1995));

(v) Check cashing and wire transmission services (*Midland Bank, PLC,* 76 Federal Reserve Bulletin 860 (1990) (check cashing); *Norwest Corporation,* 81 Federal Reserve Bulletin 1130 (1995) (money transmission));

(vi) In connection with offering banking services, providing notary public services, selling postage stamps and postage-paid envelopes, providing vehicle registration services, and selling public transportation tickets and tokens (*Popular, Inc.,* 84 Federal Reserve Bulletin 481 (1998)); and

(vii) Real estate title abstracting (*The First National Company,* 81 Federal Reserve Bulletin 805 (1995)).

(b) *Activities determined to be usual in connection with the transaction of banking abroad.* Any activity that the Board had determined by regulation in effect on November 11, 1999, to be usual in connection with the transaction of banking or other financial operations abroad (*see* §211.5(d) of this chapter), subject to the terms and conditions in part 211 and Board interpretations in effect on that date regarding the scope and conduct of the activity. In addition to the activities listed in paragraphs (a) and (c) of this section, these activities are:

(1) Providing management consulting services, including to any person with respect to nonfinancial matters, so long as the management consulting services are advisory and do not allow the financial holding company to control the person to which the services are provided;

(2) Operating a travel agency in connection with financial services offered by the financial holding company or others; and

(3) Organizing, sponsoring, and managing a mutual fund, so long as:

(i) The fund does not exercise managerial control over the entities in which the fund invests; and

(ii) The financial holding company reduces its ownership in the fund, if any, to less than 25 percent of the equity of the fund within one year of sponsoring the fund or such additional period as the Board permits.

(c) *Activities permitted under section 4(k)(4) of the BHC Act* (12 U.S.C. 1843(k)(4)). Any activity defined to be financial in nature under sections 4(k)(4)(A) through (E), (H) and (I) of the BHC Act (12 U.S.C. 1843(k)(4)(A) through (E), (H) and (I)).

(d) *Activities determined to be financial in nature or incidental to financial activities by the Board*—

(1) *Acting as a finder*—Acting as a finder in bringing together one or more buyers and sellers of any product or service for transactions that the parties themselves negotiate and consummate.

(i) *What is the scope of finder activities?* Acting as a finder includes providing any or all of the following services through any means—

(A) Identifying potential parties, making inquiries as to interest, introducing and referring potential parties to each other, and arranging contacts between and meetings of interested parties;

(B) Conveying between interested parties expressions of interest, bids, offers, orders and confirmations relating to a transaction; and

(C) Transmitting information concerning products and services to potential parties in connection with the activities described in paragraphs (d)(1)(i)(A) and (B) of this section.

(ii) *What are some examples of finder services?* The following are examples of the services that may be provided by a finder when done in accordance with paragraphs (d)(1)(iii) and (iv) of this section. These examples are not exclusive.

(A) Hosting an electronic marketplace on the financial holding company's Internet web site by providing hypertext or similar links to the web sites of third party buyers or sellers.

(B) Hosting on the financial holding company's servers the Internet web site of—

(*1*) A buyer (or seller) that provides information concerning the buyer (or seller) and the products or services it seeks to buy (or sell) and allows sellers (or buyers) to submit expressions of interest, bids, offers, orders and confirmations relating to such products or services; or

(*2*) A government or government agency that provides information concerning the services or benefits made available by the government or government agency, assists persons in completing applications to receive such services or benefits from the government or agency, and allows persons to transmit their applications for services or benefits to the government or agency.

(C) Operating an Internet web site that allows multiple buyers and sellers to exchange information concerning the products and services that they are willing to purchase or sell, locate potential counterparties for transactions, aggregate orders for goods or services with those made by other parties, and enter into transactions between themselves.

(D) Operating a telephone call center that provides permissible finder services.

(iii) What limitations are applicable to a financial holding company acting as a finder?

(A) A finder may act only as an intermediary between a buyer and a seller.

(B) A finder may not bind any buyer or seller to the terms of a specific transaction or negotiate the terms of a specific transaction on behalf of a buyer or seller, except that a finder may—

(*1*) Arrange for buyers to receive preferred terms from sellers so long as the terms are not negotiated as part of any individual transaction, are provided generally to customers or broad categories of customers, and are made available by the seller (and not by the financial holding company); and

(*2*) Establish rules of general applicability governing the use and operation of the finder service, including rules that—

(*i*) Govern the submission of bids and offers by buyers and sellers that use the finder service and the circumstances under which the finder service will match bids and offers submitted by buyers and sellers; and

(*ii*) Govern the manner in which buyers and sellers may bind themselves to the terms of a specific transaction.

(C) A finder may not—

(*1*) Take title to or acquire or hold an ownership interest in any product or service offered or sold through the finder service;

(*2*) Provide distribution services for physical products or services offered or sold through the finder service;

(*3*) Own or operate any real or personal property that is used for the purpose of manufacturing, storing, transporting, or assembling physical products offered or sold by third parties; or

(*4*) Own or operate any real or personal property that serves as a physical location for the physical purchase, sale or distribution of products or services offered or sold by third parties.

(D) A finder may not engage in any activity that would require the company to register or obtain a license as a real estate agent or broker under applicable law.

(iv) *What disclosures are required?* A finder must distinguish the products and services offered by the financial holding company from those offered by a third party through the finder service.

(2) [Reserved]

(e) *Activities permitted under section 4(k)(5) of the Bank Holding Company Act (12 U.S.C. 1843(k)(5)).*

(1) The following types of activities are financial in nature or incidental to a financial activity when conducted pursuant to a determination by the Board under paragraph (e)(2) of this section:

(i) Lending, exchanging, transferring, investing for others, or safeguarding financial assets other than money or securities;
(ii) Providing any device or other instrumentality for transferring money or other financial assets; and
(iii) Arranging, effecting, or facilitating financial transactions for the account of third parties.

(2) Review of specific activities—
(i) *Is a specific request required?* A financial holding company that wishes to engage on the basis of paragraph (e)(1) of this section in an activity that is not otherwise permissible for a financial holding company must obtain a determination from the Board that the activity is permitted under paragraph (e)(1).
(ii) *Consultation with the Secretary of the Treasury.* After receiving a request under this section, the Board will provide the Secretary of the Treasury with a copy of the request and consult with the Secretary in accordance with section 4(k)(2)(A) of the Bank Holding Company Act (12 U.S.C. 1843(k)(2)(A)).
(iii) *Board action on requests.* After consultation with the Secretary, the Board will promptly make a written determination regarding whether the specific activity described in the request is included in an activity category listed in paragraph (e)(1) of this section and is therefore either financial in nature or incidental to a financial activity.

(3) *What factors will the Board consider?* In evaluating a request made under this section, the Board will take into account the factors listed in section 4(k)(3) of the BHC Act (12 U.S.C. 1843(k)(3)) that it must consider when determining whether an activity is financial in nature or incidental to a financial activity.

(4) *What information must the request contain?* Any request by a financial holding company under this section must be in writing and must:
(i) Identify and define the activity for which the determination is sought, specifically describing what the activity would involve and how the activity would be conducted; and
(ii) Provide information supporting the requested determination, including information regarding how the proposed activity falls into one of the categories listed in paragraph (e)(1) of

this section, and any other information required by the Board concerning the proposed activity.

APPENDIX E. AFFILIATED TRANSACTIONS

Federal Reserve Act § 23A (12 U.S.C. § 371c)

(a) Restrictions on transactions with affiliates.

(1) A member bank and its subsidiaries may engage in a covered transaction with an affiliate only if—

(A) in the case of any affiliate, the aggregate amount of covered transactions of the member bank and its subsidiaries will not exceed 10 per centum of the capital stock and surplus of the member bank; and

(B) in the case of all affiliates, the aggregate amount of covered transactions of the member bank and its subsidiaries will not exceed 20 per centum of the capital stock and surplus of the member bank.

(2) For the purpose of this section, any transaction by a member bank with any person shall be deemed to be a transaction with an affiliate to the extent that the proceeds of the transaction are used for the benefit of, or transferred to, that affiliate.

(3) A member bank and its subsidiaries may not purchase a low-quality asset from an affiliate unless the bank or such subsidiary, pursuant to an independent credit evaluation, committed itself to purchase such asset prior to the time such asset was acquired by the affiliate.

(4) Any covered transactions and any transactions exempt under subsection (d) of this section between a member bank and an affiliate shall be on terms and conditions that are consistent with safe and sound banking practices.

(b) Definitions

For the purpose of this section—

(1) the term "affiliate" with respect to a member bank means—

(A) any company that controls the member bank and any other company that is controlled by the company that controls the member bank;

(B) a bank subsidiary of the member bank;

(C) any company—

(i) that is controlled directly or indirectly, by a trust or otherwise, by or for the benefit of shareholders who beneficially or otherwise control, directly or indirectly, by trust or otherwise, the member bank or any company that controls the member bank; or

(ii) in which a majority of its directors or trustees constitute a majority of the persons holding any such office with the member bank or any company that controls the member bank;

(D)

(i) any company, including a real estate investment trust, that is sponsored and advised on a contractual basis by the member bank or any subsidiary or affiliate of the member bank; or

(ii) any investment company with respect to which a member bank or any affiliate thereof is an investment advisor as defined in section 80a–2 (a)(20) of title 15 [Investment Company Act of 1940]; and

(E) any company that the Board determines by regulation or order to have a relationship with the member bank or any subsidiary or affiliate of the member bank, such that covered transactions by the member bank or its subsidiary with that company may be affected by the relationship to the detriment of the member bank or its subsidiary; and

(2) the following shall not be considered to be an affiliate:

(A) any company, other than a bank, that is a subsidiary of a member bank, unless a determination is made under paragraph (1)(E) not to exclude such subsidiary company from the definition of affiliate;

(B) any company engaged solely in holding the premises of the member bank;

(C) any company engaged solely in conducting a safe deposit business;

(D) any company engaged solely in holding obligations of the United States or its agencies or obligations fully guaranteed by the United States or its agencies as to principal and interest; and

(E) any company where control results from the exercise of rights arising out of a bona fide debt previously contracted, but only for the period of time specifically authorized under applicable State or Federal law or regulation or, in the absence of such law or regulation, for a period of two years from the date of the exercise of such rights or the effective date of this Act, whichever date is later, subject, upon application, to authorization by the Board for good cause shown of extensions of time for not more than one year at a time, but such extensions in the aggregate shall not exceed three years;

(3)

(A) a company or shareholder shall be deemed to have control over another company if—

(i) such company or shareholder, directly or indirectly, or acting through one or more other persons owns, controls, or has power to vote 25 per centum or more of any class of voting securities of the other company;

(ii) such company or shareholder controls in any manner the election of a majority of the directors or trustees of the other company; or

(iii) the Board determines, after notice and opportunity for hearing, that such company or shareholder, directly or indirectly, exercises a controlling influence over the management or policies of the other company; and

(B) notwithstanding any other provision of this section, no company shall be deemed to own or control another company by virtue of its ownership or control of shares in a fiduciary capacity, except as provided in paragraph (1)(C) of this subsection or if the company owning or controlling such shares is a business trust;

(4) the term "subsidiary" with respect to a specified company means a company that is controlled by such specified company;

(5) the term "bank" includes a State bank, national bank, banking association, and trust company;

(6) the term "company" means a corporation, partnership, business trust, association, or similar organization and, unless specifically excluded, the term "company" includes a "member bank" and a "bank";

(7) the term "covered transaction" means with respect to an affiliate of a member bank—
  (A) a loan or extension of credit to the affiliate;
  (B) a purchase of or an investment in securities issued by the affiliate;
  (C) a purchase of assets, including assets subject to an agreement to repurchase, from the affiliate, except such purchase of real and personal property as may be specifically exempted by the Board by order or regulation;
  (D) the acceptance of securities issued by the affiliate as collateral security for a loan or extension of credit to any person or company; or
  (E) the issuance of a guarantee, acceptance, or letter of credit, including an endorsement or standby letter of credit, on behalf of an affiliate;
(8) the term "aggregate amount of covered transactions" means the amount of the covered transactions about to be engaged in added to the current amount of all outstanding covered transactions;
(9) the term "securities" means stocks, bonds, debentures, notes, or other similar obligations; and
(10) the term "low-quality asset" means an asset that falls in any one or more of the following categories:
  (A) an asset classified as "substandard", "doubtful", or "loss" or treated as "other loans especially mentioned" in the most recent report of examination or inspection of an affiliate prepared by either a Federal or State supervisory agency;
  (B) an asset in a nonaccrual status;
  (C) an asset on which principal or interest payments are more than thirty days past due; or
  (D) an asset whose terms have been renegotiated or compromised due to the deteriorating financial condition of the obligor.
(11) Rebuttable presumption of control of portfolio companies.—In addition to paragraph (3), a company or shareholder shall be presumed to control any other company if the company or shareholder, directly or indirectly, or acting through 1 or more other persons, owns or controls 15 percent or more of the equity capital of the other company pursuant to subparagraph (H) or (I) of section 1843 (k)(4) of this title or rules adopted under section 122 of the Gramm-Leach-Bliley Act, if any, unless the company

or shareholder provides information acceptable to the Board to rebut this presumption of control.

(c) Collateral for certain transactions with affiliates.

(1) Each loan or extension of credit to, or guarantee, acceptance, or letter of credit issued on behalf of, an affiliate by a member bank or its subsidiary shall be secured at the time of the transaction by collateral having a market value equal to—

(A) 100 per centum of the amount of such loan or extension of credit, guarantee, acceptance, or letter of credit, if the collateral is composed of—

(i) obligations of the United States or its agencies;

(ii) obligations fully guaranteed by the United States or its agencies as to principal and interest;

(iii) notes, drafts, bills of exchange or bankers' acceptances that are eligible for rediscount or purchase by a Federal Reserve Bank; or

(iv) a segregated, earmarked deposit account with the member bank;

(B) 110 per centum of the amount of such loan or extension of credit, guarantee, acceptance, or letter of credit if the collateral is composed of obligations of any State or political subdivision of any State;

(C) 120 per centum of the amount of such loan or extension of credit, guarantee, acceptance, or letter of credit if the collateral is composed of other debt instruments, including receivables; or

(D) 130 per centum of the amount of such loan or extension of credit, guarantee, acceptance, or letter of credit if the collateral is composed of stock, leases, or other real or personal property.

(2) Any such collateral that is subsequently retired or amortized shall be replaced by additional eligible collateral where needed to keep the percentage of the collateral value relative to the amount of the outstanding loan or extension of credit, guarantee, acceptance, or letter of credit equal to the minimum percentage required at the inception of the transaction.

(3) A low-quality asset shall not be acceptable as collateral for a loan or extension of credit to, or guarantee, acceptance, or letter of credit issued on behalf of, an affiliate.

(4) The securities issued by an affiliate of the member bank shall not be acceptable as collateral for a loan or extension of credit to, or guarantee, acceptance, or letter of credit issued on behalf of, that affiliate or any other affiliate of the member bank.

(5) The collateral requirements of this paragraph shall not be applicable to an acceptance that is already fully secured either by attached documents or by other property having an ascertainable market value that is involved in the transaction.

(d) Exemptions.

The provisions of this section, except subsection (a)(4) of this section, shall not be applicable to—

(1) any transaction, subject to the prohibition contained in subsection (a)(3) of this section, with a bank—

(A) which controls 80 per centum or more of the voting shares of the member bank;

(B) in which the member bank controls 80 per centum or more of the voting shares; or

(C) in which 80 per centum or more of the voting shares are controlled by the company that controls 80 per centum or more of the voting shares of the member bank;

(2) making deposits in an affiliated bank or affiliated foreign bank in the ordinary course of correspondent business, subject to any restrictions that the Board may prescribe by regulation or order;

(3) giving immediate credit to an affiliate for uncollected items received in the ordinary course of business;

(4) making a loan or extension of credit to, or issuing a guarantee, acceptance, or letter of credit on behalf of, an affiliate that is fully secured by—

(A) obligations of the United States or its agencies;

(B) obligations fully guaranteed by the United States or its agencies as to principal and interest; or

(C) a segregated, earmarked deposit account with the member bank;

(5) purchasing securities issued by any company of the kinds described in section 1843 (c)(1) of this title;

(6) purchasing assets having a readily identifiable and publicly available market quotation and purchased at that market quotation or, subject to the prohibition contained in subsection (a)(3) of this

section, purchasing loans on a nonrecourse basis from affiliated banks; and

(7) purchasing from an affiliate a loan or extension of credit that was originated by the member bank and sold to the affiliate subject to a repurchase agreement or with recourse.

(e) Rules relating to banks with financial subsidiaries.

(1) Financial subsidiary defined.

For purposes of this section and section 371c–1 of this title, the term "financial subsidiary" means any company that is a subsidiary of a bank that would be a financial subsidiary of a national bank under section 24a of this title.

(2) Financial subsidiary treated as an affiliate.

For purposes of applying this section and section 371c–1 of this title, and notwithstanding subsection (b)(2) of this section or section 371c–1 (d)(1) of this title, a financial subsidiary of a bank—

(A) shall be deemed to be an affiliate of the bank; and

(B) shall not be deemed to be a subsidiary of the bank.

(3) Exceptions for transactions with financial subsidiaries.

(A) Exception from limit on covered transactions with any individual financial subsidiary

Notwithstanding paragraph (2), the restriction contained in subsection (a)(1)(A) of this section shall not apply with respect to covered transactions between a bank and any individual financial subsidiary of the bank.

(B) Exception for earnings retained by financial subsidiaries.

Notwithstanding paragraph (2) or subsection (b)(7) of this section, a bank's investment in a financial subsidiary of the bank shall not include retained earnings of the financial subsidiary.

(4) Anti-evasion provision.

For purposes of this section and section 371c–1 of this title—

(A) any purchase of, or investment in, the securities of a financial subsidiary of a bank by an affiliate of the bank shall be considered to be a purchase of or investment in such securities by the bank; and

(B) any extension of credit by an affiliate of a bank to a financial subsidiary of the bank shall be considered to be an extension of credit by the bank to the financial subsidiary if the Board determines that such treatment is necessary or appropriate to prevent evasions of this chapter and the Gramm-Leach-Bliley Act.

(f) Rulemaking and additional exemptions.
  (1) The Board may issue such further regulations and orders, including definitions consistent with this section, as may be necessary to administer and carry out the purposes of this section and to prevent evasions thereof.
  (2) The Board may, at its discretion, by regulation or order exempt transactions or relationships from the requirements of this section if it finds such exemptions to be in the public interest and consistent with the purposes of this section.
  (3) Rulemaking required concerning derivative transactions and intraday credit.—
    (A) In general.—Not later than 18 months after November 12, 1999, the Board shall adopt final rules under this section to address as covered transactions credit exposure arising out of derivative transactions between member banks and their affiliates and intraday extensions of credit by member banks to their affiliates.
    (B) Effective date.—The effective date of any final rule adopted by the Board pursuant to subparagraph (A) shall be delayed for such period as the Board deems necessary or appropriate to permit banks to conform their activities to the requirements of the final rule without undue hardship.

Federal Reserve Act § 23B (12 U.S.C. § 371c-1)

(a) In general.
  (1) Terms.
  A member bank and its subsidiaries may engage in any of the transactions described in paragraph (2) only—
    (A) on terms and under circumstances, including credit standards, that are substantially the same, or at least as favorable to such bank or its subsidiary, as those prevailing at the time for comparable transactions with or involving other nonaffiliated companies, or

(B) in the absence of comparable transactions, on terms and under circumstances, including credit standards, that in good faith would be offered to, or would apply to, nonaffiliated companies.

(2) Transactions covered.

Paragraph (1) applies to the following:

(A) Any covered transaction with an affiliate.

(B) The sale of securities or other assets to an affiliate, including assets subject to an agreement to repurchase.

(C) The payment of money or the furnishing of services to an affiliate under contract, lease, or otherwise.

(D) Any transaction in which an affiliate acts as an agent or broker or receives a fee for its services to the bank or to any other person.

(E) Any transaction or series of transactions with a third party—

(i) if an affiliate has a financial interest in the third party, or

(ii) if an affiliate is a participant in such transaction or series of transactions.

(3) Transactions that benefit affiliate.

For the purpose of this subsection, any transaction by a member bank or its subsidiary with any person shall be deemed to be a transaction with an affiliate of such bank if any of the proceeds of the transaction are used for the benefit of, or transferred to, such affiliate.

(b) Prohibited transactions.

(1) In general.

A member bank or its subsidiary—

(A) shall not purchase as fiduciary any securities or other assets from any affiliate unless such purchase is permitted—

(i) under the instrument creating the fiduciary relationship,

(ii) by court order, or

(iii) by law of the jurisdiction governing the fiduciary relationship; and

(B) whether acting as principal or fiduciary, shall not knowingly purchase or otherwise acquire, during the existence of any underwriting or selling syndicate, any security if a principal underwriter of that security is an affiliate of such bank.

(2) Exception.

Subparagraph (B) of paragraph (1) shall not apply if the purchase or acquisition of such securities has been approved, before such securities are initially offered for sale to the public, by a majority of the directors of the bank based on a determination that the purchase is a sound investment for the bank irrespective of the fact that an affiliate of the bank is a principal underwriter of the securities.

(3) Definitions.

For the purpose of this subsection—

(A) the term "security" has the meaning given to such term in section 78c (a)(10) of title 15 [Securities Exchange Act of 1934]; and

(B) the term "principal underwriter" means any underwriter who, in connection with a primary distribution of securities—

(i) is in privity of contract with the issuer or an affiliated person of the issuer;

(ii) acting alone or in concert with one or more other persons, initiates or directs the formation of an underwriting syndicate; or

(iii) is allowed a rate of gross commission, spread, or other profit greater than the rate allowed another underwriter participating in the distribution.

(c) Advertising restriction.

A member bank or any subsidiary or affiliate of a member bank shall not publish any advertisement or enter into any agreement stating or suggesting that the bank shall in any way be responsible for the obligations of its affiliates.

(d) Definitions.

For the purpose of this section—

(1) the term "affiliate" has the meaning given to such term in section 371c of this title (but does not include any company described in section (b)(2) of such section or any bank);

(2) the terms "bank", "subsidiary", "person", and "security" (other than security as used in subsection (b) of this section) have the meanings given to such terms in section 371c of this title; and

(3) the term "covered transaction" has the meaning given to such term in section 371c of this title (but does not include any

transaction which is exempt from such definition under subsection (d) of such section).

(e) Regulations.

The Board may prescribe regulations to administer and carry out the purposes of this section, including—

(1) regulations to further define terms used in this section; and

(2) regulations to—

(A) exempt transactions or relationships from the requirements of this section; and

(B) exclude any subsidiary of a bank holding company from the definition of affiliate for purposes of this section,

if the Board finds such exemptions or exclusions are in the public interest and are consistent with the purposes of this section.

End Notes

[1] P.L. 106-102.

[2] Technically, the GSA is the same as the Banking Act of 1933; however, the GSA has come to refer to only four sections (§§ 16, 20, 21, and 32) of that piece of legislation, 48 Stat. 162.

[3] There are three primary types of federal depository charters: bank, thrift (a.k.a., savings and loan association), and credit union. Thrifts, like banks, offer federally insured consumer deposits, but thrifts, unlike banks, historically have been mission-oriented through a required focus on residential mortgages and related assets. In order to maintain this concentration, thrifts have been subject to limitations on the types of assets in which they can invest. Credit unions engage in activities similar to those of banks and thrifts, but usually on a more limited basis. Credit unions, unlike most banks and thrifts, are owned by their depositors and are tax-exempt. *The Department of the Treasury Blueprint for a Modernized Financial Regulatory Structure*, Dept. of Treasury, pp. 38-39, Mar. 2008, available at http://ustreas.gov/ press/releases/reports/Blueprint.pdf. This chapter focuses on banks.

[4] 70 Stat. 133.

[5] 48 Stat. 74, codified at 15 U.S.C. §§ 77a *et seq.*

[6] Another important bar to banks' dealing in securities is the BHCA, administered by the Board of Governors of the Federal Reserve System (FRB). Prior to enactment of the GLBA, the BHCA prohibited companies owning or controlling banks (i.e., bank holding companies (BHCs)), from acquiring "ownership or control ... of any company which is not a bank or ... any company the activities of which had been determined by the ... [FRB] to be so closely related to banking as to be a proper incident thereto." 12 U.S.C. § 1843.

[7] Charles K, Whitehead, *Reframing Financial Regulation*, 90 B.U. L. Rev. 1, 5 (2010).

[8] Strong competition between the various types of depository institutions, as well as between state and federally chartered depositories, and by extension, the various regulators overseeing these institutions continues to exist in the financial services industry. See, Elizabeth F. Brown, *"E Pluribus Unum"—Out of Many, One: Why the United States Needs a Single Financial Services Agency*, 14 U. Miami Bus. L. Rev. 1 (2005).

[9] *Id.* at 16-36.

[10] A "bank holding company" (BHC) is defined to mean, in pertinent part, "any company which has control over any bank." 12 U.S.C. § 1841(a)(1).

[11] In addition to these, the Office of Thrift Supervision (OTS) is the primary federal regulator for federal thrifts and some thrift holding companies on a consolidated basis. For more information on the regulation of financial companies, see CRS Report R40249, *Who Regulates Whom? An Overview of U.S. Financial Supervision*, by Mark Jickling and Edward V. Murphy.

[12] 12 Stat. 665.

[13] 12 U.S.C. § 24(Seventh) (stating , in part: "To exercise ... all such incidental powers as shall be necessary to carry on the business of banking; by discounting and negotiating promissory notes, drafts, bills of exchange, and other evidences of debt; by receiving deposits; by buying and selling exchange, coin, and bullion; by loaning money on personal security; and by obtaining, issuing, and circulating notes according to the provisions of title 62 of the Revised Statutes.").

[14] See, e.g., 12 U.S.C. § 1828.

[15] See, e.g., 12 U.S.C. § 1820(d).

[16] 12 U.S.C. § 1831o; 12 U.S.C. § 1818.

[17] 12 U.S.C. § 1821. See also CRS Report RL34657, *Financial Institution Insolvency: Federal Authority over Fannie Mae, Freddie Mac, and Depository Institutions*, by David H. Carpenter and M. Maureen Murphy.

[18] The discount window is the Federal Reserve's authority to lend directly to depository institutions and U.S branches of foreign banks, generally where the depository is unable to acquire funding in the private market. Loans made through the discount window must be sufficiently collateralized and are subject to a interest rate above the federal funds rate. 12 U.S.C. § 343. For more information on the discount window, see *Federal Reserve Discount Window*, Federal Reserve System, available at *http://www.frbdiscountwindow.org* /discountwindowbook.cfm?hdrID=14&dtlID= 43.

[19] See, generally, CRS Report R40783, *Hedge Funds: Legal Status and Proposals for Regulation*, by Kathleen Ann Ruane and Michael V. Seitzinger.

[20] CRS Report RS22581, *Overview of Major Federal Securities Laws*, by Michael V. Seitzinger.

[21] See, supra discussion of GSA § 21. See, also, David M. Eaton, *The Commercial Banking-Related Activities of Investment Banks and Other Nonbanks*, 44 Emory L. J. 1187 (1995).

[22] However, in emergency situations, there are two possible ways investment banks may secure credit from the Federal Reserve banks. If they are able to offer U.S. government issued or guaranteed obligations as collateral for their own promissory notes and the Federal Reserve bank, in consultation with the FRB, judges that credit is unavailable elsewhere and that failure to secure credit would have an adverse effect on the U.S. economy, advances may be granted to such individuals, partnerships, or corporations. If they lack adequate eligible security for advances, Section 13(3) of the Federal Reserve Act (FRA) provides a mechanism by which a discount may be secured upon the vote of five or more Members of the FRB. 12 U.S.C. § 343. The applicable Board Regulation, 12 C.F.R. § 201.4(d) reads:

> *Emergency credit for others.* In unusual and exigent circumstances and after consultation with the Board of Governors, a Federal Reserve Bank may extend credit to an individual, partnership, or corporation that is not a depository institution if, in the judgment of the Federal Reserve Bank, credit is not available from other sources and failure to obtain such credit would adversely affect the economy. If the collateral used to secure emergency credit consists of assets other than obligations of, or fully guaranteed as to principal and interest by, the United States or an agency thereof, credit must be in the form of a discount and five or more members of the Board of Governors must affirmatively vote to authorize the discount prior to the extension of credit. Emergency credit will be extended at a rate above the highest rate in effect for advances to depository institutions.

[23] SEC Press Release, *Chairman Cox Announces End of Consolidated Supervised Entities Program*, Sept. 26, 2008, available at http://www.sec.gov/news/press/2008/2008-230.htm.

[24] 15 U.S.C. § 78q(i).

[25] *Id.*

[26] Directive 2002/87/EC of the European Parliament and of the Council (16 December 2002). http://eur-lex.europa.eu/ LexUriServ/LexUriServ.do?uri=CELEX:32002L0087:EN:HTML.

[27] 12 U.S.C. § 335. Section 5(c) of the Banking Act of 1933, 48 Stat. 165, subjected state-chartered banks to the same securities limitations that GSA imposed on national banks, using the following language: "[s]tate member banks shall be subject to the same limitations and conditions with respect to the purchasing, selling, underwriting, and holding of investment securities and stock as are applicable in the case of national banks."

[28] 12 U.S.C. § 24(Seventh); 12 C.F.R. § 1.3(a)(1).

[29] 12 U.S.C. § 24(Seventh); Securities Industry Association v. Board of Governors, 807 F. 2d 1052 (D.C. Cir. 1986), *cert. denied*, 483 U.S. 1005 (1987).

[30] 12 U.S.C. § 24(Seventh).

[31] Under 12 U.S.C. § 24(Seventh) "investment securities" is defined to "mean marketable obligations, evidencing indebtedness of any person, copartnership, association, or corporation in the form of bonds, notes and/or debentures commonly known as investment securities under such further definition of the term 'investment securities' as may by regulation be prescribed by the Comptroller of the Currency."

[32] 12 C.F.R. § 1.2(e). The regulation does not define "speculative in nature." This requirement was included in the regulations promulgated by OCC on December 2, 1996, 61 Fed. Reg. 63972, implementing the Secondary Mortgage Market Enhancement Act of 1984, P.L. 98-440, 98 Stat. 1691, and the Riegle Community Development and Regulatory Improvement Act of 1994, P.L. 103-325, 108 Stat. 2162, modifying GSA section 16, to remove quantitative limits on national bank investments in certain mortgage-backed and small business loan-backed securities subject to OCC regulations. It appears that OCC determined that by requiring that these types of securities be of investment grade and "marketable" under 12 C.F.R. §§ 1.2(l) and 1.2(m) "ensures that national banks do not acquire asset-backed securities that have speculative characteristics." 61 Fed. Reg. at 63975 and 63976.

[33] 17 C.F.R. § 239,144A.

[34] 12 C.F.R. § 1.2(f).

[35] 12 U.S.C. § 24(Seventh); 12 C.F.R. § 1.3.

[36] 12 U.S.C. § 221a(b) defines "affiliate" in terms of various indices of control, such as ownership of 50 percent of the voting shares of the company.

[37] 12 U.S.C. §§ 1843(a)(1) and (c)(8). One notable exception to this restriction was that the BHCA, as originally enacted, did not cover holding companies owning only a single bank. This exception was removed by the Bank Holding Company Act Amendments of 1970. P.L. 91-607.

[38] Jerry W. Markham, *Banking Regulation: Its History and Future*, 4 N.C. Banking Inst. 221, 240-44 (2000).

[39] Alan E. Sorcher and Satish M. Kini, *Does the Term "Bank Broker-Dealer" Still Have Meaning?*, 6 N.C. Banking Inst. 227, 233-34 (2002). See, also, Charles K. Whitehead, *Reframing Financial Regulation*, 90 B.U. L. Rev. 1, 17-18 (2010).

[40] Securities Industry Assoc. v. Comptroller of the Currency, 577 F.Supp. 252, 255 (D.C. Cir. 1985) (internal citations omitted) (quoting Letter from James E. Smith, Comptroller of the Currency, to G. Duane Vieth (June 10, 1974), reprinted in [1973-78] Fed. Banking L. Rep. (CCH ¶ 96,272)).

[41] 401 U.S. 617 (1971).

[42] *Id.* at 626-27.

[43] *Id.* at 628.

[44] *Id.* at 630.

[45] The Court refers to "subtle hazards," presumably as a contrast with the obvious hazard of a bank's investing its own funds imprudently, which according to the Court, had not been a danger even in the 1920s because banks had been operating securities activities through separate affiliates that had no ready access to bank assets. *Id.* at 630.

[46] *Id.* at 630.

[47] *Id.* at 630-34.

[48] *Id.* at 635-39.

[49] Deference towards agency interpretation was further spurred by the landmark 1984 Supreme Court decision in *Chevron, U.S.A., Inc. v. Natural Resources Defense Council, Inc.* in which the Court held that reviewing courts, in the absence of clear legislative language to the contrary, shall uphold agency interpretations that are reasonable. 467 U.S. 837 (1984).

[50] Saule T. Omarova, *The Quiet Metamorphosis: How Derivatives Changed the "Business of Banking"*, 63 U. Miami L. Rev. 1041, 1052 (2009).

[51] 513 U.S. 251, 258 fn. 2 (1995).

[52] OCC Interpretive Letter No. 684 (Aug. 4, 1995).

[53] OCC Interpretative Letter No. 380 (Dec. 29, 1986), *reprinted* in Banking L. Rep. CCH ¶ 85, 604 (considered an "incidental" power).

[54] OCC Interpretative Letter No. 380 (Dec. 29, 1986) (*citing* an "unpublished letter from J.T. Watson, Deputy Comptroller of the Currency, July 11, 1975 (membership on commodities exchange permitted for bank operating subsidiary executing transactions for bank's own account)," among other unpublished letters).

[55] Securities Industry Assoc. v. Comptroller of the Currency, 577 F.Supp. 252 (D.C. Cir. 1985). The court described discount brokerage this way: [The bank subsidiaries will be] "discount" brokerages, which will buy and sell securities solely as agent, on the order and for the account of customers. Neither will purchase or sell securities for its own account, nor engage in underwriting, nor give investment advice. "Discount" brokers are so characterized because their commissions are significantly lower than those charged by full-service brokers who, in addition to trading on behalf of customers, offer investment advice. *Id.* at 253.

[56] OCC Interpretative Letter No. 386 (June 10, 1987), *reprinted* in Banking L. Rep. CCH ¶ 85,610.

[57] OCC Interpretative Letter No. 380 (Dec. 29, 1986) (*stating*: "It is an established practice for national banks to lend either their own investment or trading account securities, or their customers' securities held in custody, safekeeping, trust, or pension accounts.").

[58] Investment Co. Institute v. Clarke, 630 F.Supp. 593 (D.Conn. 1986).

[59] 73 Fed. Res. Bull. 2, fn. 43 (1987) (citing OCC, FDIC, FRB, *Commercial Bank Private Placement Activities* (1978)).

[60] OCC Interpretative Letter No. 380 (Dec. 29, 1986). *reprinted* in Banking L. Rep. CCH ¶ 85, 604.

[61] *Eligibility of Securities for Purchase, Dealing In Underwriting and Holding by National Banks; Rulings Issued by the Comptroller*, OCC, 47 Fed. Reg. 18,323 (Apr. 29, 1982).

[62] OCC Interpretive Letter No. 652 (Sept. 13, 1994). The letter defined "equity derivative swaps" this way:

> Equity derivative swap contracts are notional principal contracts which provide for equity based bilateral payments. Notional principal contracts ("NPCs") are financial instruments under which one party, in exchange for a specified consideration, makes payments to the counterparty at designated intervals. The amount of the payment made to the counterparty is calculated by reference to a specified index and is based upon a notional principal investment in that index. With the exception of certain currency swaps, the parties to a NPC never exchange the notional investment amount. Rather, the notional investment is used only as a reference for determining the amount of payments to be transferred. ... The parties to an equity derivative swap contract agree to make payments to one another based on an increase or decrease in

> the value of a notional principal investment in a particular equity or equity index. One party (the "short") agrees to make periodic payments to the counterparty (the "long") if there is an increase in the value of the notional principal investment. The short also agrees to pay the long amounts equal to dividends on the equity or equity index. The long agrees to make periodic payments to the short based on a specified floating rate of interest applied to the same notional principal investment. In addition, the long agrees to make payments to the short if there is any decrease in the value of the notional investment in the equity or index.

Id. at 2-3.

[63] Comptroller of the Currency, Risk Management of Financial Derivatives: Comptroller's Handbook, at 64 (1997), available at http://www.occ.treas.gov/handbook/deriv.pdf.

[64] OCC Interpretive Letter No. 892 (Sept. 13, 2000), available at *http://www.occ* .gov/interp/sep00/int892.pdf, *stating*:

> In brief, the OCC determined, in the case of three national banks, that the banks could take positions in equity securities solely to hedge bank permissible equity derivative transactions originated by customers for their valid and independent business purposes. The banks committed that they will use equities solely for hedging and not for speculative purposes. The banks will not take anticipatory, or maintain residual positions in equities except as necessary to the orderly establishment or unwinding of a hedging position. Moreover, the banks may not acquire equities for hedging purposes that constitute more than 5% of a class of stock of any issuer.

Id. at 1. The OCC describes the hedging transaction this way:

> Currently, the banks enter into bank permissible, customer-driven equity derivative transactions that they book directly. The banks hedge the equity derivative transactions with equity derivatives or through mirror transactions with nonbank affiliates. The terms of the "mirror" transactions between the banks and nonbank affiliates exactly offset the terms of customer driven equity derivative transactions. The affiliates hedge the mirror transactions by taking physical positions in equities.
>
> To illustrate, in a "long" equity swap transaction with a customer, the bank agrees to pay the customer the appreciation, over a set period of time, in the value of a notional principal investment in the underlying equity. The bank may also agree to pay the customer amounts equal to dividends on the underlying equity. In return, the customer agrees to pay the bank if there is any decrease in value of the notional principal investment in the underlying equity, and an agreed upon rate of interest applied to that investment.
>
> The bank hedges its long swap transaction by entering into a mirror transaction with a nonbank affiliate. Under the mirror transaction, the nonbank affiliate agrees to pay the bank the appreciation in, and dividends on, the same notional principal investment in the same underlying equity under the same terms as the bank's initial transaction with the customer. The bank, in turn, agrees to pay the nonbank affiliate depreciation in, and the rate of interest applied to, the value of the underlying equity. The nonbank affiliate then hedges its obligations to the bank by purchasing the equity in an amount equal to the notional principal investment in that equity under the swap transaction between the bank and the customer. The banks represent that engaging in customer-driven equity derivative transactions in this fashion effectively moves revenues from the banks to the relevant nonbank affiliate. The banks prefer to eliminate the "mirror" portion of their equity derivative transactions and internally book the physical hedges.

Id. at 2-3 (internal citations omitted).

[65] 516 F. 2d 1229, (D.C. Cir. 1975).

[66] *Id.*, at 1237.

[67] 49 Fed. Reg. 794, 806 (Jan. 5, 1984).

[68] See, e.g., Securities Industry Association v. Board of Governors of the Federal Reserve System, 468 U.S. 137 (1984); Securities Industry Association v. Board of Governors of the Federal Reserve System, 900 F. 2d 360 (D.C. Cir. 1990); Securities Industry Association v. Board of Governors of the Federal Reserve System, 839 F.2d 47 (2d Cir. 1988), *cert. denied*, 486 U.S. 1059 (1988); Securities Industry Association v Board of Governors of the Federal Reserve System, 847 F. 2d 890 (D.C. Cir. 1988); Securities Industry Association v. Board of Governors of the Federal Reserve System, 807 F. 2d 1052 (D.C. Cir. 1986), *cert denied*, 483 U.S. 1005 (1987).

[69] Orders Issued Under Section 4 of the Bank Holding Company Act, Citicorp, J.P. Morgan & Co. Incorporated, and Bankers Trust New York Corporation, Order Approving Applications to Engage in Limited Underwriting and Dealing in Certain Securities, 73 Fed. Res. Bull. 473 (1987). The FRB "concluded that subsidiaries would not be engaged substantially in bank-ineligible activities if no more than five to ten percent of their total gross revenues was derived from such activities over a two-year period, and if the activities in connection with *each* type of bank-ineligible security did not constitute more than five to ten percent of the market for that particular security." Securities Industry Assoc. v. Board of Governors, 839 F.2d 47, 51 (2nd Cir. 1988) [emphasis original], *citing* Bankers Trust New York Corp., 73 Fed. Reserve Bull. 138, 485-86 (1987).

[70] Revenue Limit on Bank-Ineligible Activities of Subsidiaries of Bank Holding Companies Engaged in Underwriting and Dealing in Securities, 61 Fed. Reg. 68,750, 68,752 (Dec. 30, 1996), *effective* Mar. 6, 1997..

[71] Some commenters to the FRB's proposed regulations, which were largely adopted as part of the final regulations, argued that increasing the gross revenue threshold to 25% would allow commercial banks "to affiliate with the nation's largest investment banks, contrary to the express purpose of section 20 of the Glass-Steagall Act." The FRB responded by stating:

> although not relevant to the statutory interpretation, the Board is not convinced that a 25 percent revenue limit would allow unlimited affiliation between banks and investment banks for purposes of section. Adverse commenters provided no data to support their assertion that it would. The Board has reviewed the publicly available financial information for a sample of the largest investment banks, and it is not apparent that they would be in compliance with a 25 percent revenue limit. ... Determining the ineligible revenue of independent investment banks is difficult because they do not segregate ineligible revenue from eligible revenue in their annual reports or the FOCUS reports that they file with the Securities Exchange Commission.

61 Fed. Reg. 68,755 and 68,755, fn. 32 (Dec. 30, 1996).

[72] Alan E. Sorcher and Satish M. Kini, *Does the Term "Bank Broker-Dealer" Still Have Meaning*, 6 N.C. Bank. Inst., 227, 232 (2002).

[73] 61 Fed. Reg. 68,754-55 (Dec. 30, 1996). The regulations stated:

> The Board has concluded that the 10 percent revenue limit unduly restricts the underwriting and dealing activity of section 20 subsidiaries to a level that falls short of "principal engagement'' for purposes of section 20. This conclusion is based on the Board's experience with the section 20 subsidiaries through the process of examination and supervision. The conclusion is also supported by identifiable changes in the relationship between gross revenue and underwriting and dealing activity since the Board's 1987 Order.

61 Fed. Reg. 68,753 (Dec. 30, 1996).

[74] 61 Fed. Reg. 68,750-51 (Dec. 30, 1996), citing Citicorp, J.P. Morgan & Co., and Bankers Trust New York Corp., 73 Fed. Res. Bull. 473 (1987), aff'd, Securities Industry Ass'n v. Board of Governors, 839 F.2d 47, 66 (2d Cir.), cert. denied, 486 U.S. 1059 (1988); Chemical New York Corp., Chase Manhattan Corp., Bankers Trust New York Corp., Citicorp, Manufacturers Hanover Corp., and Security Pacific Corp., 73 Federal Reserve Bulletin 731 (1987); J.P. Morgan & Co., The Chase Manhattan Corp., Bankers Trust New York Corp.,

Citicorp, and Security Pacific Corp., 75 Federal Reserve Bulletin 192 (1989), aff'd, Securities Industries Ass'n v. Board of Governors, 900 F.2d 360 (D.C. Cir. 1990).

[75] Board of Governors for the Federal Reserve System v. Investment Company Institute, 450 U.S. 46 (1981).

[76] Securities Industry Assoc. v. Board of Governors for the Federal Reserve System, 468 U.S. 207 (1984).

[77] It includes activities related to extending credit; real estate appraising; check-guaranty services; collection agency services; credit bureau services; asset management, real estate settlement services; operating industrial loan companies and savings associations; management consulting; employee benefits consulting; career counseling; courier services; various limited insurance services; community development activities; money orders; and data processing.

[78] Jerry W. Markham, *Banking Regulation: Its History and Future*, 4 N.C. Banking Inst. 221, 269-70 (2000).

[79] See, e.g., S. 100-1886, the Proxmire Financial Modernization Act of 1988, which passed the Senate; and H.Rept. 104-1062, the Financial Services Competiveness Act of 1995, which was marked up and reported favorably from both the House Committee on Banking and Financial Services and the House Committee on Commerce.

[80] P.L. 106-102, 113 Stat. 1338.

[81] P.L. 106-102, § 101, 113 Stat. 1341.

[82] P.L. 84-511, 70 Stat. 1333, 12 U.S.C. §§ 1841 *et seq.*

[83] P.L. 106-102, § 102, 113 Stat. 1338, 1341-1342. Prior to enactment of the GLBA, a BHC was not permitted to engage in any activities other than (1) banking or (2) activities that the FRB has found to be "so closely related to banking ... as to be a proper incident thereto." Providing insurance as a principal, agent, or broker was explicitly excluded from that category of activities. 12 U.S.C. § 1843(c)(8) (1994 ed.). The FRB, however, in the years before the enactment of the GLBA, issued rulings that were viewed as eroding legal barriers to insurance activities by BHCs by administrative action rather than by legislation. See, e.g., Merchants National Corp., 73 Fed. Res. Bull. 876 (September 10, 1987); Independent Insurance Agents of America v. Federal Reserve Board, 838 F. 2d 627 (2d Cir. 1988); Merchants National Corp., 75 Fed. Res. Bull. 388 (1989); and, Independent Insurance Agents of America v. Federal Reserve Board, 890 F. 2d 1275 (2d Cir. 1989).

[84] Under 12 U.S.C. § 1843(k)(4)(B), as amended by the GLBA, FHCs may engage in "[i]nsuring, guaranteeing, or indemnifying against loss, harm, damage, illness, disability, or death, or providing and issuing annuities, and acting as a principal, agent, or broker for purposes of the foregoing, in any State."

[85] P.L. 106-102, § 103, 113 Stat. 1342, 12 U.S.C. § 1843(k). A "bank holding company" is defined to mean, in pertinent part, "any company which has control over any bank." 12 U.S.C. § 1841(a)(1).

[86] 12 U.S.C. § 335. Section 5(c) of the Banking Act of 1933, 48 Stat. 165, subjected state-chartered banks to the same securities limitations that the GSA imposed on national banks, using the following language: "[s]tate member banks shall be subject to the same limitations and conditions with respect to the purchasing, selling, underwriting, and holding of investment securities and stock as are applicable in the case of national banks."

[87] See "The Glass-Steagall Act" section of this chapter.

[88] 12 U.S.C. § 378.

[89] For more information on this issue, see the "Regulation of Commercial Banks and Securities Firms" section of this chapter.

[90] Under the Savings and Loan Holding Company Act (S&LHCA), 12 U.S.C. § 1467a, a savings and loan holding company (S&LHC) is a company which controls a savings association (or thrift) and is, thereby, subject to the registration, examination, supervision, and activities restrictions of the S&LHCA as administered by the Office of Thrift Supervision (OTS). These restrict S&LHCs from engaging in activities not authorized for federal savings

associations or for BHCs under the BHCA, 12 U.S.C. §§ 1841 *et seq.* as amended by the GLBA. These activities restrictions do not apply to grandfathered unitary thrift holding companies (i.e., companies owning only one thrift or savings association). The GLBA generally eliminated the advantages which had permitted unitary thrift holding companies to engage in a full range of securities activities as well as in commercial activities. However, the GLBA grandfathered certain institutions—unitary thrift holding companies in existence on May 4, 1999, as well as those, such as AIG, which, on May 4, 1999, had pending an application to acquire a thrift. 12 U.S.C. §467a(c)(9)(C).

[91] 12 U.S.C.§ 1467a(c)(9).

[92] 12 U.S.C. § 1843(k)(1).

[93] 12 U.S.C. § 1843(k)(4).

[94] 12 C.F.R. § 225.28.

[95] 12 U.S.C. §§ 1843(k)(1) – (3).

[96] 12 U.S.C. § 1843(l)(1). There is also an additional requirement applicable to any expansion of activities—that all insured depository affiliates have received a satisfactory rating under the most recent Community Reinvestment Act examination. 12 U.S.C. § 1843(l)(2).

[97] 12 U.S.C. §§ 1844(c)(2)(D) and (E).

[98] 12 U.S.C. § 1844(c)(4) (securities and insurance activities of subsidiaries of banks); 15 U.S.C. §§ 78c(a)(4); 78c(a)(5); 78o-3, 78c, note; 80a-17(f); 80a-17(f); 80a(2)(a)(6); 80a(2)(a)(11); and 80b(2)(a)(11)(A) (replacing the broad exemption from the securities laws accorded to banks prior to passage of the GLBA).

[99] 12 U.S.C. §§ 1844(c)(1) – (3).

[100] *See* Mark B. Greenlee, *Historical Review of 'Umbrella Supervision' by the Board of Governors of the Federal Reserve System*, 27 Rev. Banking & Fin. L. 407, 433-458 (2008).

[101] 15 U.S.C. § 78q(i).

[102] 12 U.S.C. § 1844(c)(2)(A).

[103] 12 U.S.C. § 1844(c)(2)(C), as added by P.L. 106-102, § 111, 113 Stat. 1338, 1364. This provision reads:

(C) Restricted focus of examinations. The Board shall, to the fullest extent possible, limit the focus and scope of any examination of a bank holding company to—
(i) the bank holding company; and
(ii) any subsidiary of the bank holding company that could have a materially adverse effect on the safety and soundness of any depository institution subsidiary of the holding company due to—
(I) the size, condition, or activities of the subsidiary; or
(II) the nature or size of transactions between the subsidiary and any depository institution that is also a subsidiary of the bank holding company.

[104] 12 U.S.C. §§ 1848a(a) – (c). That statute reads, in pertinent part:

(a)Thc Board may not prescribe regulations, issue or seek entry of orders, impose restraints, restrictions, guidelines, requirements, safeguards, or standards, or otherwise take any action under or pursuant to any provision of this Act or section 8 of the Federal Deposit Insurance Act [12 U.S.C. § 1818] against or with respect to a functionally regulated subsidiary of a bank holding company unless—
(1) the action is necessary to prevent or redress an unsafe or unsound practice or breach of fiduciary duty by such subsidiary that poses a material risk to—
(A) the financial safety, soundness, or stability of an affiliated depository institution; or
(B) the domestic or international payment system; and
(2) the Board finds that it is not reasonably possible to protect effectively against the material risk at issue through action directed at or against the affiliated depository institution or against depository institutions generally.
(b) Limitation on indirect action. The Board may not prescribe regulations, issue or seek entry of orders, impose restraints, restrictions, guidelines, requirements,

safeguards, or standards, or otherwise take any action under or pursuant to any provision of this Act or section 8 of the Federal Deposit Insurance Act [12 U.S.C. § 1818] against or with respect to a bank holding company that requires the bank holding company to require a functionally regulated subsidiary of the holding company to engage, or to refrain from engaging, in any conduct or activities unless the Board could take such action directly against or with respect to the functionally regulated subsidiary in accordance with subsection (a).

(c) Actions specifically authorized. Notwithstanding subsection (a) or (b), the Board may take action under this Act or section 8 of the Federal Deposit Insurance Act [12 U.S.C. § 1818] to enforce compliance by a functionally regulated subsidiary of a bank holding company with any Federal law that the Board has specific jurisdiction to enforce against such subsidiary.

[105] 12 U.S.C. § 1844(c).

[106] 12 U.S.C. § 1844(c)(1).

[107] 12 U.S.C. § 1844(c)(2)(C). The provision reads:

The Board shall, to the fullest extent possible, forego an examination by the Board under this paragraph and instead review the reports of examination made of—

(i) any registered broker or dealer by or on behalf of the Securities and Exchange Commission;

(ii) any registered investment adviser properly registered by or on behalf of either the Securities and Exchange Commission or any State;

(iii) any licensed insurance company by or on behalf of any State regulatory authority responsible for the supervision of insurance companies; and

(iv) any other subsidiary that the Board finds to be comprehensively supervised by a Federal or State authority.

[108] 12 U.S.C. § 1844(c)(2)(A).

[109] 12 U.S.C. § 1844(c)(2)(B). This provision reads:

Notwithstanding subparagraph (A), the Board may make examinations of a functionally regulated subsidiary of a bank holding company only if—

(i) the Board has reasonable cause to believe that such subsidiary is engaged in activities that pose a material risk to an affiliated depository institution;

(ii) the Board reasonably determines, after reviewing relevant reports, that examination of the subsidiary is necessary to adequately inform the Board of the systems described in subparagraph (A)(ii)(II); or

(iii) based on reports and other available information, the Board has reasonable cause to believe that a subsidiary is not in compliance with this Act or any other Federal law that the Board has specific jurisdiction to enforce against such subsidiary, including provisions relating to transactions with an affiliated depository institution, and the Board cannot make such determination through examination of the affiliated depository institution or the bank holding company.

[110] 12 U.S.C. § 1844(c)(2)(C).

[111] 12 U.S.C. § 1844(c)(3)(A).

[112] 12 U.S.C. §§ 1844(g)(1) and (2).

[113] 12 U.S.C. §§ 1844(g)(3) and (4).

[114] 12 U.S.C. § 1844(e)

[115] For further information on merchant banking, see Valentine V. Craig, *Merchant Banking Past and Present*, 14 FDIC Banking Review (2001), available at *http://www.fdic.gov/bank* /analytical/banking/2001sep/article2.html.

[116] 12 U.S.C. § 24a (a)(2)(A).

[117] 12 U.S.C. § 1831w. Essentially, the same conditions apply to state banks as are applicable to national banks with respect to controlling a financial subsidiary. State-chartered banks may conduct "activities that are financial in nature" only if the bank and each of its insured depository affiliates are well capitalized after making the capital deductions dictated for

national banks under 12 U.S.C. § 24a(c); the bank complies with the financial and operating standards set for the national banks under 12 U.S.C. § 24a(d); and there is compliance with the restrictions on transactions with affiliates found in section 23A and 23B of the Federal Reserve Act, 12 U.S.C. §§ 371c and 371c-1.

[118] 12 U.S.C. § 24(Seventh); 12 C.F.R. § 1.3.

[119] 12 U.S.C. § 24(Seventh); Sec. Indus. Ass'n v. Bd. of Governors, 807 F. 2d 1052 (D.C. Cir. 1986), *cert. denied*, 483 U.S. 1005 (1987).

[120] 12 U.S.C. § 24(Seventh).

[121] Under 12 U.S.C. § 24(Seventh) "investment securities" is defined to "mean marketable obligations, evidencing indebtedness of any person, copartnership, association, or corporation in the form of bonds, notes and/or debentures commonly known as investment securities under such further definition of the term 'investment securities' as may by regulation be prescribed by the Comptroller of the Currency."

[122] 12 U.S.C. § 24a(a)(2)(B).

[123] The GLBA prohibition on merchant banking activities by financial subsidiaries of banks was absolute for the first five years after the GLBA's enactment; thereafter, the FRB and the Secretary of the Treasury have the power jointly to issue rules to permit merchant banking. 12 U.S.C. § 1843 note. To date, no such rules have been issued.

[124] The factors include marketplace and technology changes, and competitive considerations. 12 U.S.C. §§ 1843(k)(3) and (3) and 24a(b), as added by P.L. 106-102, § 103 and 121, 113 Stat. 1338, 1343 and 1374.

[125] 12 U.S.C. §§ 2901 *et seq.*

[126] 12 U.S.C. §§ 24a(a)(2) and (3). The statute provides:

> (2) Conditions and requirements. A national bank may control a financial subsidiary, or hold an interest in a financial subsidiary, only if—...
> (B) the activities engaged in by the financial subsidiary as a principal do not include—
> (i) insuring, guaranteeing, or indemnifying against loss, harm, damage, illness, disability, or death (except to the extent permitted under section 302 or 303(c) of the Gramm-Leach-Bliley Act [15 USCS § 6712 or § 6713(c)]) or providing or issuing annuities the income of which is subject to tax treatment under section 72 of the Internal Revenue Code of 1986 [26 USCS § 72];
> (ii) real estate development or real estate investment activities, unless otherwise expressly authorized by law; or
> (iii) any activity permitted in ... [12 USCS § 1843(k)(4)] [expanded activities available to FHCs], except activities described in section ... [12 USCS § 1843(k)(4)(H)] [merchant banking activities] that may be permitted in accordance with ...[12 USCS § 1843 note] ....
> (C) the national bank and each depository institution affiliate of the national bank are well capitalized and well managed;
> (D) the aggregate consolidated total assets of all financial subsidiaries of the national bank do not exceed the lesser of—
> (i) 45 percent of the consolidated total assets of the parent bank; or
> (ii) $ 50,000,000,000;
> (E) except as provided in paragraph (4), the national bank meets any applicable rating or other requirement set forth in paragraph (3); and
> (F) the national bank has received the approval of the Comptroller of the Currency for the financial subsidiary to engage in such activities, which approval shall be based solely upon the factors set forth in this section.
> (3) Rating or comparable requirement.
> (A) In general. A national bank meets the requirements of this paragraph if—

(i) the bank is 1 of the 50 largest insured banks and has not fewer than 1 issue of outstanding eligible debt that is currently rated within the 3 highest investment grade rating categories by a nationally recognized statistical rating organization; or
(ii) the bank is 1 of the second 50 largest insured banks and meets the criteria set forth in clause (i) or such other criteria as the Secretary of the Treasury and the Board of Governors of the Federal Reserve System may jointly establish by regulation and determine to be comparable to and consistent with the purposes of the rating required in clause (i).
(B) Consolidated total assets. For purposes of this paragraph, the size of an insured bank shall be determined on the basis of the consolidated total assets of the bank as of the end of each calendar year.

[127] 12 U.S.C. § 1832w.

[128] 12 U.S.C. § 24a(d).

[129] 12 U.S.C. §24a(e).

[130] 12 U.S.C. § 1828a.

[131] 12 U.S.C. §§ 371c and 371c-1.

[132] 12 U.S.C. §§ 371c(b); 371c-1(d)(1).

[133] 12 U.S.C.§ 371c(b)(7); 12 C.F.R. § 223.3(h).

[134] 12 C.F.R. § 371c.

[135] 12 U.S.C. § 1828(j)(1) (state-chartered, FDIC-insured banks); 12 U.S.C. § 1468(a) (insured savings banks).

[136] 12 U.S.C. §§ 371c(a)(1)(A) and (B).

[137] 12 U.S.C. § 371c(e)(3). Under 12 U.S.C. § 24a(a)(1) there is no limit on the interest that a national bank may hold in a financial subsidiary. This applies to state-chartered banks, as well. 12 U.S.C. § 1828(j)(1) (state-chartered, FDIC-insured banks); 12 U.S.C. § 1468(a) (insured savings banks).

[138] 12 U.S.C. § 371c(a)(3).

[139] 12 C.F.R. § 371c-1.

[140] 12 U.S.C. § 371c(e).

[141] The statute requires that such transactions must be "on terms and under circumstances, including credit standards, that ... are at least as favorable to such bank ... as those prevailing at the time for comparable with or involving other nonaffiliated companies, or ... in the absence of comparable transactions, on terms and under circumstances, including credit standards, that in good faith would be offered to, or would apply, to nonaffiliated companies." 12 U.S.C. § 371c-1(a) (1).

[142] 12 U.S.C. § 371c-1(a)(2).

[143] 12 U.S.C. §§ 371c(f)(2), 371c-1(2)(B). Under section 23B, the FRB also has authority to exclude a BHC subsidiary from the definition of "affiliate," and, therefore, from coverage under the section.

[144] 12 U.S.C. § 371c(f).

[145] 12 C.F.R., Part 223.

[146] 12 C.F.R. §§ 223.13 (terms and conditions must meet safe banking practices); 223.14 (collateral ranges from 100% of the covered transactions when collateral is U.S. agency obligations to 130% if the collateral is stock, leases, or other real or personal property; securities issued by an affiliate are ineligible as collateral).

[147] 12 C.F.R. § 223.16 (general rule: any transaction to the extent that its proceeds benefit an affiliate; exceptions include riskless principal transactions; brokerage commissions; agency fees; preexisting lines of credit; and general purpose credit card transactions).

[148] 12 C.F.R. §§ 223.21 - 223.24.

[149] 12 C.F.R. §§ 223.41 – 223.43. There are exemptions from the collateral and quantitative limits for transactions with a depository institution in which the bank controls 80% of the voting securities or with a depository institution in the same holding company if the holding company controls 80% of the voting securities of both banks; there are also exemptions for

loan purchases from an depository affiliate on a nonrecourse basis and for internal corporate reorganizations under certain circumstances. 12 C.F.R. § 223.41. There also are exemptions, under specified conditions, from those limits and from the prohibition on acquiring low-quality assets for the following types of situations; correspondent banking deposits; transactions secured by cash or U.S. government securities; purchases of securities of a servicing affiliate; purchases of certain liquid assets; purchases of marketable securities; purchases of municipal securities; purchases of extensions of credit originally sold to the affiliate under a repurchase agreement; asset purchases of a newly formed member banks; transactions approved under the Bank Merger Act, 12 U.S.C. § 1828(c); purchases of extensions of credit from an affiliate meeting certain conditions, including an independent evaluation by the bank before the affiliate grants the credit that the borrower is creditworthy; and intraday extensions of credit. 12 C.F.R. § 223.42.

[150] 12 C.F.R. § 223.43(a).

[151] 12 U.S.C. §§ 371c-1(b)(1) and (2).

[152] 12 U.S.C. § 371c-1(b)(1).

[153] 12 U.S.C. § 371c-1(b)(3).

[154] 12 U.S.C. § 1843(k)(4)(H).

[155] 12 C.F.R. §§ 225. 170 – 225.177, promulgated in 66 Fed. Reg. 8466, 8484 (January 31, 2001).

[156] 12 C.F.R. § 225.170(f).

[157] 12 C.F.R. § 225.170(a).

[158] 12 C.F.R. § 225.170(b).

[159] The regulation states that "[a] financial holding company may own or control shares, assets and ownership interests pursuant to this subpart only for a period of time to enable the sale or disposition thereof on a reasonable basis consistent with the financial viability of the financial holding company's merchant banking investment." 12 C.F.R. § 225.172(a).

[160] 12 C.F.R. § 225.172(b)(1).

[161] 12 C.F.R. § 225.170(c).

[162] 12 C.F.R.§ 225.170(d).

[163] 12 C.F.R. § 225.170(e)(1). In addition, there are requirements applicable to the books and records and separate management of the portfolio company. 12 C.F.R. §§ 225.170(e)(2) and (3).

[164] Federal Reserve System Bank Holding Company Supervision Manual § 3907.0.2.3.2, available at http://www.federalreserve.gov/boarddocs/supmanual/bhc/bhc.pdf (stating: "'portfolio company' means any company or entity that is directly or indirectly held, owned, or controlled by a FHC that is using the merchant banking authority, and the company or entity is engaged in an activity that is not authorized for the FHC under section 4 of the BHC Act.").

[165] 12 C.F.R. § 225.171(b)(f).

[166] 12 C.F.R. § 225.171.

[167] 12 C.F.R. §§ 225.171(b)(i) and (ii).

[168] 12 C.F.R. § 225.171(b)(e)(2).

[169] 12 C.F.R. § 225.171(b)(e)(1).

[170] 12 CC.F.R. 225.174(a) sets this level at the lesser of 30% of Tier 1 capital of the FHC or 20% of Tier 1 after investments in private equity funds are excluded.

[171] 12 C.F.R. § 225.173(a).

[172] 12 C.F.R. §§ 225.173(a)(2) - (5).

[173] 12 C.F.R. § 225.173(c).

[174] 12 C.F.R. § 225.173(d)(4). "Control" is determined based on such factors as: serving in certain capacities in managing the fund; owning or controlling 25% of a class of voting shares of the fund; or selecting or controlling a majority of the directors of the private equity fund. 12 C.F.R. § 225.173(a)(4).

[175] 12 C.F.R. § 225.176(b).

[176] 12 C.F.R. § 225.176(b)(3).

[177] Fed. Reserve Bd., Supervisory Guidance on Equity Investment and Merchant Banking Activities of Financial Holding Companies, and Other Banking Organizations Supervised by the Federal Reserve (June 22, 2000), available at *http://www.federalreserve.gov/boa* rddocs/SRLetters/2000/sr0009a1.pdf.

[178] *Id.*, at 13. These are described as "risk management issues [which] may arise when a banking institution or an affiliate lends to or has other business relationships with: ... a portfolio company; ... the general partner or manager of a private equity fund that has also invested in a portfolio company; or ... a private equity-financed company in which the banking institution does not hold a direct or indirect ownership interest but is an investment or portfolio company of a general partner or fund manager with which the banking organization has other investments."

[179] *Id.*, at 13.

[180] Asset management services include acting as agent in the liquidation or sale of loans and collateral for loans, including real estate and other assets acquired through foreclosure or in satisfaction of debts previously contracted.

[181] For this purpose, the divestiture period for property begins on the date that the debt is acquired, regardless of when legal title to the property is acquired.

[182] For purposes of this section, real estate settlement services do not include providing title insurance as principal, agent, or broker.

[183] The requirement that the lease be on a nonoperating basis means that the bank holding company may not, directly or indirectly, engage in operating, servicing, maintaining, or repairing leased property during the lease term. For purposes of the leasing of automobiles, the requirement that the lease be on a nonoperating basis means that the bank holding company may not, directly or indirectly: (1) Provide servicing, repair, or maintenance of the leased vehicle during the lease term; (2) purchase parts and accessories in bulk or for an individual vehicle after the lessee has taken delivery of the vehicle; (3) provide the loan of an automobile during servicing of the leased vehicle; (4) purchase insurance for the lessee; or (5) provide for the renewal of the vehicle's license merely as a service to the lessee where the lessee could renew the license without authorization from the lessor. The bank holding company may arrange for a third party to provide these services or products.

[184] Feasibility studies do not include assisting management with the planning or marketing for a given project or providing general operational or management advice.

[185] A bank-ineligible security is any security that a State member bank is not permitted to underwrite or deal in under 12 U.S.C. 24 and 335.

[186] A company or its affiliates may not enter quotes for specific bank-ineligible securities in any dealer quotation system in connection with the company's riskless principal transactions; except that the company or its affiliates may enter "bid" or "ask" quotations, or publish "offering wanted" or "bid wanted" notices on trading systems other than NASDAQ or an exchange, if the company or its affiliate does not enter price quotations on different sides of the market for a particular security during any two-day period.

[187] A bank-ineligible security is any security that a state member bank is not permitted to underwrite or deal in under 12 U.S.C. 24 and 335.

[188] This reference does not include acting as a dealer in options based on indices of bank-ineligible securities when the options are traded on securities exchanges. These options are securities for purposes of the federal securities laws and bank-ineligible securities for purposes of section 20 of the Glass-Steagall Act, 12 U.S.C. 337. Similarly, this reference does not include acting as a dealer in any other instrument that is a bank-ineligible security for purposes of section 20. A bank holding company may deal in these instruments in accordance with the Board's orders on dealing in bank-ineligible securities.

[189] In performing this activity, bank holding companies are not authorized to perform tasks or operations or provide services to client institutions either on a daily or continuing basis, except as necessary to instruct the client institution on how to perform such services for

itself. See also the Board's interpretation of bank management consulting advice (12 CFR 225.131).

[190] *Financial organization* refers to insured depository institution holding companies and their subsidiaries, other than nonbanking affiliates of diversified savings and loan holding companies that engage in activities not permissible under section 4(c)(8) of the Bank Holding Company Act (12 U.S.C. 1842(c)(8)).

[191] See also the Board's interpretation on courier activities (12 CFR 225.129), which sets forth conditions for bank holding company entry into the activity.

[192] *Extension of credit* includes direct loans to borrowers, loans purchased from other lenders, and leases of real or personal property so long as the leases are nonoperating and full-payout leases that meet the requirements of paragraph (b)(3) of this section.

[193] *Finance company* includes all non-deposit-taking financial institutions that engage in a significant degree of consumer lending (excluding lending secured by first mortgages) and all financial institutions specifically defined by individual states as finance companies and that engage in a significant degree of consumer lending.

[194] These limitations increase at the end of each calendar year, beginning with 1982, by the percentage increase in the Consumer Price Index for Urban Wage Earners and Clerical Workers published by the Bureau of Labor Statistics.

[195] Nothing contained in this provision shall preclude a bank holding company subsidiary that is authorized to engage in a specific insurance-agency activity under this clause from continuing to engage in the particular activity after merger with an affiliate, if the merger is for legitimate business purposes and prior notice has been provided to the Board.

[196] For the purposes of this paragraph, activities engaged in on May 1, 1982, include activities carried on subsequently as the result of an application to engage in such activities pending before the Board on May 1, 1982, and approved subsequently by the Board or as the result of the acquisition by such company pursuant to a binding written contract entered into on or before May 1, 1982, of another company engaged in such activities at the time of the acquisition.

In: Banks, Securities and the Volcker Rule… ISBN: 978-1-61761-988-5
Editors: Nicole A. Garcia

Chapter 2

THE "VOLCKER RULE": PROPOSALS TO LIMIT "SPECULATIVE" PROPRIETARY TRADING BY BANKS

David H. Carpenter and M. Maureen Murphy

SUMMARY

In 1933, during the first 100 days of President Franklin D. Roosevelt's New Deal, the Securities Act of 1933 and the Glass-Steagall Act (GSA) were enacted, setting up a pervasive regulatory scheme for the public offering of securities and generally prohibiting commercial banks from underwriting and dealing in those securities. Banks are subject to heavy, expensive prudential regulation, while the regulation of securities firms is predominately built around registration, disclosure of risk, and the prevention and prosecution of insider trading and other forms of fraud.

While there are two distinct regulatory systems, the distinguishing lines between the traditional activities engaged in by commercial and investment banks became increasingly difficult to discern as a result of competition, financial innovation, and technological advances in combination with permissive agency and judicial interpretation.

One of the benefits of being a bank, and thus being subject to more extensive regulation, is access to what is referred to as the "federal safety net," which includes the Federal Deposit Insurance Corporation's (FDIC's) deposit insurance, the Federal Reserve's discount window lending facility, and the Federal Reserve's payment system.

In the wake of the Great Recession of 2008, there have been calls to reexamine the activities that should be permissible for commercial banks in light of the fact that they receive governmental benefits through access to the federal safety net. Some have called for the reenactment of the provisions of the GSA that imposed affiliation restrictions between banks and securities firms, which were repealed by the Gramm-Leach-Bliley Act (GLBA) in 1999.

While neither the House- nor the Senate-passed version of H.R. 4173, the comprehensive financial regulatory reform proposals of the 111th Congress, includes provisions that would reenact the GSA, both bills do propose curbs on "proprietary trading" by banking institutions. H.R. 4173, newly titled the Dodd-Frank Wall Street Reform and Consumer Protection Act, which is modeled on the Senate version, would limit the ability of commercial banking institutions and their affiliated companies and subsidiaries to engage in trading unrelated to customer needs and investing in and sponsoring hedge funds or private equity funds. Such an approach has been referred to as the "Volcker Rule," having been urged upon Congress by Paul Volcker, former Chairman of the Board of Governors for the Federal Reserve System and current Chairman of the President's Economic Recovery Advisory Board.

This chapter briefly discusses the permissible proprietary trading activities of commercial banks and their subsidiaries under current law. It then analyzes the Volcker Rule proposals under the House- and Senate-passed financial reform bills and under the Conference Report. **Appendix A**, **Appendix B**, and **Appendix C** of the report provide the full legislative language in each.

INTRODUCTION

In 1933, during the first 100 days of President Franklin D. Roosevelt's New Deal, the Securities Act of 1933[1] and the Glass-Steagall Act (GSA)[2] were enacted, setting up a pervasive regulatory scheme for the public offering of securities and generally prohibiting commercial banks from underwriting and dealing in those securities.[3] GSA prohibited affiliations between banks (which, for the purposes of this chapter, means bank-chartered depository institutions, that is, financial institutions that hold federally insured consumer deposits) and securities firms (which are commonly referred to as "investment banks" even though they are not technically banks and do not hold federally insured consumer deposits);[4] further restrictions on bank affiliations with non-banking firms were enacted in Bank Holding Company Act of 1956 (BHCA)[5] and its subsequent amendments, eliminating the possibility that companies owning banks would be permitted to take ownership or controlling interest in insurance companies, manufacturing companies, real estate companies, securities firms, or any other non-banking company. As a result, distinct regulatory systems developed in the United States for regulating banks, on the one hand, and securities firms on the other.

Banks are institutions of limited power; they may only engage in the activities permissible pursuant to their charter, which generally limits them to the "business of banking" and all powers incidental to the business of banking.[6] Included in these activities restrictions are certain limitations on their ability to engage in proprietary trading, that is, investing as principal, rather than at the behest or for the benefit of customers, for the bank's own account. In addition to activity restrictions, banks are subject to capital standards, affiliation restrictions, management interlocking restrictions, and many other standards;[7] they are subject to regular examinations to ensure they are being well-managed, conducting business in a safe and sound fashion, and complying with numerous consumer protection and other laws;[8] and federal banking regulators have a full range of strong and flexible enforcement tools, such as prompt corrective action powers, to rectify problems that are found during examinations.[9]

One of the benefits of being a bank, and thus being subjected to heavy, expensive regulation, is access to what is referred to as the "federal safety net," which includes the Federal Deposit Insurance Corporation's (FDIC's) deposit insurance, the Federal Reserve's discount window lending facility,[10] and the Federal Reserve's payment system.

The regulation and oversight of securities firms are very different from that of banks. Securities firms may be primarily regulated by the Securities and Exchange Commission (SEC) at the federal level, or they may not be regulated directly at the federal level at all, which often is the case for hedge funds, private equity firms, and special purpose vehicles (SPVs).[11] Rather than regulating for safety and soundness, the SEC's regulatory regime is predominately built around registration, disclosure of risk, and the prevention and prosecution of insider trading and other forms of fraud. SEC-regulated firms generally are not subject to capital and liquidity standards or to regular safety and soundness examinations.[12] And aside from a general prohibition on accepting federally insured consumer deposits, securities firms generally are not subject to activity restrictions, as are banks.[13] As a result, these institutions generally do not have access to the federal safety net.[14]

While there are two distinct regulatory systems, the distinguishing lines between the traditional activities engaged in by commercial and investment banks became increasingly difficult to discern as a result of competition, financial innovation, and technological advances in combination with permissive agency and judicial interpretation. Beginning in the late 1970s, the Board of Governors of the Federal Reserve System (FRB), as the primary regulator for bank holding companies (BHCs),[15] and the Office of the Comptroller of the Currency (OCC), as the primary regulator for national banks, issued a series of regulations and orders, liberally interpreting the limitations imposed on the activities of commercial banks through laws such as the GSA and the BHCA. The result was the incremental expansion of the types and levels of securities activities permissible for BHCs and financial subsidiaries of banks. The Gramm-Leach-Bliley Act of 1999 (GLBA)[16] continued this trend by repealing two of the four sections of the GSA and the BHCA and by establishing the financial holding company (FHC) structure, which permits commercial banks and full-service investment banks (as well as insurance companies) to coexist under common control.

In the wake of the Great Recession of 2008, there have been calls to reexamine the activities that should be permissible for commercial banks in light of the fact that they receive governmental benefits through access to the federal safety net. Some have called for the reenactment of the repealed provisions of the GSA, which is discussed in greater detail in another CRS report.[17]

While neither the House- nor the Senate-passed version of H.R. 4173, the comprehensive financial regulatory reform proposals of the 111th Congress, includes provisions that would reenact the GSA, both bills do propose curbs on "proprietary trading" by banking institutions. The bills would limit the ability of commercial banking institutions and their affiliated companies and subsidiaries to engage in trading unrelated to customer needs and investing in and sponsoring hedge funds or private equity funds. Such an approach has been referred to as the "Volcker Rule," having been urged upon Congress by Paul Volcker, former Chairman of the FRB and current Chairman of the President's Economic Recovery Advisory Board.

This chapter briefly discusses the permissible proprietary trading activities of commercial banks and their subsidiaries under current law. It then analyzes the Volcker Rule proposals under both the House- and Senate-passed financial reform bills. **Appendix A**, **Appendix B**, and **Appendix C** of the report provide the full legislative language from both bills.

CURRENT RESTRICTIONS ON PROPRIETARY TRADING

Pre-GLBA

The OCC and the FRB are empowered to implement, enforce, and, by extension, interpret (by regulation, guidance, or order) the subtleties and ambiguities of the GSA and the BHCA. For several decades after the enactment of the GSA, banks did not attempt to expand beyond traditional banking activities to a significant degree. This trend began to change in the 1970s. High inflation, coupled with a consumer movement to interest-bearing accounts and investment products, such as money market funds offered by securities firms, reduced the profitability of traditional bank products.[18] Corporate consumers also began moving to securities firms for short-term lending (e.g., through the commercial paper market), which, for some, was less expensive than borrowing directly from banks. Facing lower profits and stiffer competition from securities firms, banks began seeking approval from regulators to engage in a greater universe of securities activities.[19] Additionally, regulators may have become less cautious as time passed after the Great Depression.[20]

Beginning in the 1970s and 1980s, requests for approval to engage in a greater universe of securities activities were largely granted by the OCC and the FRB, and, in most cases, have been approved by courts. By the time that the GLBA was enacted in 1999, the FRB had authorized certain BHCs and their subsidiaries to underwrite and deal in an array of bank-ineligible securities, including municipal bonds, commercial paper, mortgage-backed securities and other consumer-related securities, corporate debt securities, and corporate equity securities.[21] In addition to underwriting and dealing activities, the FRB also approved other securities activities such as the provision of investment advice,[22] the brokering of securities,[23] and others. The FRB promulgated the list of permissible nonbanking activities at 12 C.F.R. § 225.28(b).[24] With respect to securities-related activities, the regulation includes two distinct categories: (1) agency functions for customers and (2) transactions as principal (i.e., for the company's own account, often referred to as "proprietary trading"). In the latter category are the following: (1)

"[u]nderwriting and dealing in government obligations and money market instruments"; (2) "[i]nvesting and trading activities" in certain swaps, futures, options, foreign exchange, and other derivative contracts; and (3) "buying and selling bullion and related activities." The FRB requires banks to adhere to a number of limitations and conditions, largely spelled out in regulation, in order to engage as principal in each of these three categories.

Post-GLBA

After GLBA, commercial banks were provided the authority to make proprietary investments in a broader array of securities, but to do so, they generally must either be organized as an FHC or the bank itself must establish a financial subsidiary. The permissible proprietary activities vary for FHCs and financial subsidiaries, so they are addressed in turn.

Financial Holding Companies

The GLBA introduced the FHC, a separate form of BHC for companies wishing to expand beyond the business of banking and closely related activities to a broader array of financial services. The GLBA permits FHCs to engage in and own companies engaging in (1) activities that are "financial in nature or incidental to such financial activity" or (2) activities that are "complementary to a financial activity" and do "not pose a substantial risk to the safety and soundness of the depository."[25] The GLBA listed certain activities as "financial in nature,"[26] including all the nonbanking activities which had already been authorized for BHCs.[27] The GLBA empowered the FRB, in coordination with the Secretary of the Treasury, to issue orders or regulations supplementing that list.[28]

Merchant Banking Investments. Under the GLBA[29] and rules promulgated jointly by the Secretary of the Treasury and the FRB,[30] FHCs with a securities affiliate or an insurance affiliate with an investment adviser affiliate[31] may engage in what is referred to as merchant banking activities, under certain conditions. Merchant banking means to "directly or indirectly and as principal or on behalf of one or more persons, ... acquire or control any amount of shares, assets or ownership interests of a company or other entity that is engaged in any activity not otherwise authorized for the financial holding company."[32] FHC merchant banking investments must be "part of a bona fide underwriting or merchant or investment banking activity."[33]

Additionally, the interests must only be held on a temporary basis[34] and, in general, no longer than 10 years.[35] Under the regulation, the shares in such investments may be acquired by any subsidiary of the FHC other than a depository institution subsidiary.[36] If assets other than debt or equity securities are involved, they must be "held or promptly transferred to a portfolio company."[37] "Portfolio company," in this context, is merely the term used for the company to which these assets must be transferred.[38] Depository institution subsidiaries of the FHC may not routinely manage the portfolio company.[39] There also are restrictions designed to prevent the FHC from routinely managing or operating the portfolio company.[40] For example, executive officers of the holding company and of certain subsidiaries of the holding company, including its securities broker and depository institution subsidiaries, may not serve as executive officers of the portfolio company.[41] Despite these restrictions, however, there is a provision which permits an FHC to routinely, but on a temporary basis,[42] manage a portfolio company; this may occur "only when intervention by the financial holding company is necessary or required to obtain a reasonable return on the financial holding company's investment in the portfolio company upon resale or other disposition of the investment, such as to avoid or address a significant operation loss or in connection with a loss of senior management at the portfolio company."[43] The FRB's prior approval is not generally required for an FHC to engage in merchant banking activities unless the proposed investment will result in the aggregate carrying value of all merchant banking investments to exceed a certain level.[44]

Merchant Banking Investments Through a Private Equity Fund. An FHC also may make merchant banking investments though a private equity fund that makes investments in nonfinancial companies, provided the private equity fund meets certain qualifications and the FHC's investments comply with requirements for merchant banking. "Private equity fund" is defined, for this purpose, as a company "formed for the purpose of and exclusively engaged in the business of investing in shares, assets, and ownership interests of financial and nonfinancial companies for resale or other disposition."[45] The private equity company must not be an operating company; no more than 25% of its equity may be held by the FHC or any of its officers, directors, employees or principal shareholders; its term must be no longer than 15 years; and it must not have been formed to evade the merchant banking restrictions on FHCs.[46] If an FHC makes investments through a private equity fund, the investments will generally be subject to a 15-year limitation rather than the 10-

year limit that would apply if the FHC were to make direct investments.[47] If an FHC controls a private equity fund, the FHC may not routinely operate the private equity fund.[48]

Federal Reserve Act (FRA) §§ 23A, which imposes limitations on "covered transactions"[49] between a bank and its affiliates, and 23B,[50] which requires certain transactions to be on market terms, apply to transactions between an FHC and its subsidiaries and the private equity fund only if control exists.[51]

The regulations presume control for applicability of sections 23A and 23B if the FHC controls more than 15% of the private equity firm's total equity.[52] This presumption may be rebutted with contrary evidence presented to the FRB or by showing the existence of any one of the following presumptions against control: (1) none of the FHC's officers, directors, or employees serves as a director or trustee of the firm; (2) another person or entity holds more of the total equity of the firm than does the FHC and no more than one of the FHC's officers, directors, or employees serves as a director or trustee of the firm; (3) another person or entity controls more than 50% of the voting shares of the firm and the officers, directors, or employees of the FHC do not constitute a majority of the directors or trustees of the firm.[53]

On June 22, 2000, the FRB issued guidance on FHCs' equity investments and merchant banking activities.[54] This guidance focuses on sound policies and practices, including board of directors oversight; limits on and controls with respect to types and amounts of investments; periodic reviews of investments and of the component elements of the investment process; assessment of possible investment performance under various circumstances; internal controls adopted to types of investments; exit strategies; and capital allocation based on risk. There are also guidelines on transactions involving the portfolio company which are not subject to the FRA §§ 23A and 23B.[55] FHCs are urged to

> have systems and policies in place to monitor transactions between the holding company, or a non-depository institution subsidiary of the holding company, and a portfolio company ... [to] assure that the risks of these transactions, including exposures of the holding company on a consolidated basis to a single portfolio company, are reasonably limited and that all transactions are on reasonable terms, with special attention paid to transactions that are not on market terms.[56]

Financial Subsidiaries of State- and Federally Chartered Banks

Since the GLBA, not only may banks affiliate with securities firms within the FHC structure, national banks and state-chartered banks also may, subject to certain conditions, own or control financial subsidiaries that may engage in many of the same securities activities permissible for FHCs. Specifically, the GLBA authorized national banks to control or hold an interest in financial subsidiaries which could engage in "activities that are financial in nature or incidental to financial activity," as well as "activities that are permitted for national banks to engage in directly (subject to the same terms and conditions that govern the conduct of the activities by a national bank)."[57] It also provided authorization for state-chartered banks to control or hold interests in subsidiaries engaging "in activities as principal that would only be permissible for a national bank to conduct through a financial subsidiary."[58]

In general, financial subsidiaries may conduct any other activities authorized for FHCs with exceptions[59] for (1) underwriting insurance or annuities, except for certain grandfathered activities primarily related to credit insurance; (2) developing or investing in real estate; and (3) merchant banking[60] or insurance portfolio investing. There is also a provision permitting the Secretary of the Treasury to designate additional activities as financial in nature, in coordination with the FRB, based on the same standards as are applicable to the FRB when adding to the list of financial activities under the BHCA.[61]

For a national bank to hold a financial subsidiary that is engaging in proprietary financial activities as principal, rather than in an agency capacity, the bank and all of its depository institution affiliates must be well capitalized; there must be OCC approval; the bank must have a satisfactory rating under the Community Reinvestment Act;[62] the assets of all financial subsidiaries of the bank must not exceed the lesser of $50 billion or 45% of the assets of the bank; and the largest banks must adhere to additional requirements.[63] State-chartered, federally insured banks have similar authority, provided that the bank and all of its insured depository institution affiliates are well capitalized and well managed.[64]

Financial Regulatory Reform: How House and Senate Versions of H.R. 4173 Treat the "Volcker Rule"

Volcker Testimony

Testifying before the Senate Committee on Banking, Housing, and Urban Affairs on February 2, 2010, Chairman Paul Volcker urged the committee to prevent commercial banking institutions, beneficiaries of taxpayer-subsidized deposit insurance and emergency liquidity, from continuing to engage in sponsoring and investing in hedge funds and private equity funds and "trading unrelated to customer needs and continuing banking relationships."[65] These activities he identified as "essentially proprietary and speculative activities."[66] Although he provided no definitions in his testimony, he made it clear that he believed that any definitional problems could be overcome by providing regulators "broad" and "specific" authority to define "hedge fund" and "private equity fund" and that regulators could use it to prevent the emergence of "a new breed of bank-based funds that in all but name would function as hedge or equity funds." He was equally optimistic about the ability of Congress and the regulators to deal with the dangers of "proprietary trading." He indicated that he thought that there are means available by which regulators could identify, and eliminate, speculative proprietary trading by bank fund managers not only because of the potential risks for the institutions but also because of possible conflicts with the interests of their customers. He described "proprietary trading," at least in terms of any sizeable volume, as being conducted by only "a handful of large commercial banks"—"maybe four or five in the United States and perhaps a couple of dozen worldwide."[67]

House Provision

H.R. 4173, as passed by the House of Representatives, addresses proprietary trading only in the context of certain companies—financial holding companies that have been determined to be systemically significant by the Financial Services Oversight Council[68] and, therefore, subjected to stricter prudential standards. Section 1117(a) of the measure provides authority for the Board of Governors of the Federal Reserve System (FRB) to ban proprietary trading by financial holding companies that have been subjected to stricter standards upon determining that such trading "poses an existing or foreseeable threat to the safety and soundness of such company or to the financial stability of the United States." The bill defines "proprietary trading" as "the trading of stocks, bonds, options, commodities, derivatives, or other financial instruments with the company's own money and for the company's own account."[69] The bill allows the FRB broad power to make exemptions to the ban. Not only may the FRB exempt proprietary trading determined to be "ancillary to other operations," such as making a market in securities, hedging risk, and determining the market value of the company's assets, the FRB may, through regulation, exempt any other type of proprietary trading.

Senate Provision

Section 619 of the Senate-passed version of H.R. 4173, which is included in the Conference Base Text of H.R. 4173,[70] requires the federal banking agencies to engage in a joint rulemaking to prohibit "proprietary trading" and investing in hedge funds or private equity funds by covered entities, that is, federally insured depository institutions, bank holding companies, companies treated as bank holding companies,[71] and their subsidiaries. Before the banking agencies conduct the rulemaking to prohibit proprietary trading and investment in hedge funds, however, the Financial Stability Oversight Council, which is substantively similar to the House bill's Financial Services Oversight Council, must conduct a study. The Council consists of nine presidentially appointed voting members; [72] it is chaired by the Secretary of the Treasury; and, pursuant to other sections of the legislation, it possesses substantive powers relating to systemic risk and regulation of financial companies. The study must be completed within six months of enactment of this legislation and is to be geared to assessing the potential implications and effect of the specifications of section 619 with respect to a list of factors, including taxpayer costs; household and business burdens; spread of the federal safety net to non-depository institutions; risk to the financial system; and safety and soundness of the institutions. On the basis of that study, the Council is required to "make recommendations" regarding the substantive prohibitions and definitions of section 619. The joint rulemaking by the banking regulators is required to "reflect any recommendations or modifications made by the Council."[73]

Subsection 619(b) of the bill requires the federal banking agencies to prohibit proprietary trading by insured depository institutions, companies directly or indirectly controlling insured depository institutions, companies treated as bank holding companies, and any of their subsidiaries (covered entities). Subsection 619(a) defines "proprietary trading" as follows:

> ... purchasing or selling, or otherwise acquiring and disposing of, stocks, bonds, options, commodities, derivatives, or other financial instruments ... for the trading book (or such other portfolio as the Federal banking agencies may determine) of such institution, company, or subsidiary ... and ... subject to such restrictions as the Federal banking agencies may determine, does not include purchasing or selling or otherwise acquiring and disposing of, stocks, bonds, options, commodities, derivatives, or other financial instruments on behalf of a customer, as part of market making activities, or otherwise in connection with or in facilitation of customer relationships, including risk-mitigating hedging activities related to such a purchase, sale, acquisition, or disposal. § 619(a)(2)

Subsection 619(b)(2) provides exceptions for the following types of obligations, provided the "investment ... is otherwise authorized by Federal law," and subject to any conditions imposed "on the conduct of investments" by the appropriate federal banking agency:

> (i) obligations of the United States or any agency of the United States, including obligations fully guaranteed as to principal and interest by the United States or an agency of the United States;
> (ii) obligations, participations, or other instruments of, or insured by, the Government National Mortgage Association, the Federal National Mortgage Association, or the Federal Home Loan Mortgage Corporation, including obligations fully guaranteed as to principal and interest by such entities; and
> (iii) obligations of any State or any political subdivision of a State.

Subsection 619(c)(1) requires the federal banking agencies to engage in a joint rulemaking procedure to prohibit the covered entities "from sponsoring or investing in a hedge fund or a private equity fund." Subsection 619(a)(1) defines "hedge fund" and "private equity fund" as "a company or other entity that is exempt from registration as an investment company pursuant to section 3(c)(1) or 3(c)(7) of the Investment Company Act of 1940 (15 U.S.C. 50a-3(c)(1) or 80a-3(c)(7)), or a similar fund, as jointly determined by the appropriate Federal banking agencies."

Under subsection 619(a)(3), "sponsoring" a hedge fund or a private equity fund includes "serving as a general partner, managing member, or trustee," "selecting ... a majority of the directors," or "sharing ... the same name or a variation of the same name" as the fund. Subsection 619(d)(1) provides exceptions from the prohibition on sponsoring or investing in a hedge fund or private equity fund for any "investment otherwise authorized under Federal law that is ... an investment in a small business investment company ... or designed primarily to promote the public welfare, as provided in" 12 U.S.C. § 24(Eleventh).[74] There are also exceptions for investments permitted under sections 4(c)(9) and 4(c)(13) of the Bank Holding Company Act,[75] provided they are conducted solely outside the United States by a company not controlled directly or indirectly by a company organized under the laws of the United States or of a state.

Subsection 619(e) prohibits covered entities that serve as investment managers or advisers to hedge funds or private equity funds from engaging in certain transactions with those funds and requires other specified transactions with them to be on market terms.[76]

Subsection 619(f) requires the FRB to "adopt rules imposing additional capital requirements and specifying additional quantitative limits for nonbank financial companies supervised by the ... [FRB] under section 113 [of the Senate legislation] that engage in proprietary trading or sponsoring and investing in hedge funds and private equity funds."[77] Excepted from these rules is a list of investments that includes U.S. obligations, obligations issued by the federal housing government-sponsored enterprises (housing GSEs), obligations of small business investment companies; state and local obligations; and obligations designed to promote the public welfare.

All of the requirements for rulemaking, regarding both proprietary trading and investments in hedge and private equity funds, are specifically subjected "to the recommendations and modifications" of the Council under subsection 619(g). Subsection (g) requires the Council to complete a study of the foregoing provisions assessing a number of factors.[78] On the basis of that study, the Council is authorized to

> make recommendations regarding the definitions ... and the implementation of [the] provisions ... including any modifications to the definitions, prohibitions, requirements, and limitations contained therein that the Council determines would more effectively implement the purposes of this section and ... make recommendations for prohibiting the conduct of the activities described ... above a specific threshold amount and imposing additional capital requirements on activities conducted below such threshold amount.

Although there are certain express exceptions to section 619's prohibitions, unlike other banking laws, section 619 does not contain a specific provision delegating broad exemptive power to the regulators.[79] It appears that, in lieu of delegating such authority to the regulators, section 619 provides the Council with some flexibility to modify the parameters of the law both by requiring the rulemaking to "reflect" Council recommendations and by including, in each of the substantive provisions defining prohibitions, language subjecting the prohibition "to the recommendations and modifications of the Council."[80] The Committee Report accompanying the bill takes a broad view of the dangers in permitting banking firms to engage in these risky activities and a narrow view of the authority of the Council to substantially alter the prohibitions of section 619.[81]

Subsections 619(g)(1)(A) and (h) present a timetable for implementation: (1) the Council is to complete its study no later than six months after the bill is enacted; (2) the regulators are to issue final rules no later than nine months after completion of the Council study; and (3) effective two years after these rules are promulgated, insured depository institutions, companies controlling depository institutions, companies treated as bank holding companies, and subsidiaries of these institutions may not retain investments or relationships prohibited under the regulations, unless a company applies for and receives an extension. Extensions may be given one year at a time for a maximum of three years for any one company.

In addition to the § 619 provisions, § 989 of the Senate-passed bill requires the Government Accountability Office to conduct a study and issue a report on "the risks and conflicts associated with proprietary trading" engaged in by banks, BHCs, FHCs, subsidiaries of BHCs and FHCs, and "any other entity, as the Comptroller General of the United States may determine." This study and report requirement also was included as part of the Conference Base Text of H.R. 4173.

The Conference Report: Section 619

Banking Entities May Not Engage in Proprietary Trading or Hedge Fund Ownership or Sponsorship; Nonbanking Financial Companies Subject to FRB Supervision May Do So With Capital and Quantitative Limits. Subsection (a) of section 619 of the Conference Report contains an outright prohibition on proprietary trading by and ownership of interests in or sponsorship of hedge funds or private equity funds by a "banking entity."

Subsequent provisions of the bill, however, provide exceptions to this. "Banking entity" is defined in subsection (h) to mean any FDIC-insured depository institution, company controlling an insured depository institution, company treated as a bank holding company for purposes of the International Banking Act of 1978, and any affiliate or subsidiary of such entity.[82] The exact language provides a broad prohibition. It reads: "a banking entity shall not … engage in proprietary trading, or … acquire or retain any equity, partnership, or other ownership interest in or sponsor a hedge fund or a private equity fund." There are, however, certain exceptions, some transitional and others designated as permitted activities under subsection (d) of the legislation.

Rather than subjecting nonfinancial companies supervised by the FRB to a prohibition on proprietary trading and hedge fund ownership or sponsorship, the legislation authorizes the regulators to issue rules subjecting such companies to additional capital and quantitative limits on such activities unless the activity has been identified as a permitted activity under section (d) and has not been subjected to capital and quantitative requirements for safety and soundness purposes.

Definitions. Subsection 619(h) sets forth definitions of various terms, in some cases providing a degree of discretion to the regulators to expand the reach of the prohibitions and limitations. For example:

> A "hedge fund" or a "private equity fund" is defined as "an issuer that would be an investment company … but for sections 3(c)(1) or 3(c)(7) of [the Investment Company Act of 1940] …, *or such similar funds as the … [appropriate regulatory agencies] may by rule … determine.*"[83]
>
> "Proprietary trading" is "engaging as principal for the trading account of the banking entity or nonbank financial company supervised by the Board in any transaction to purchase or sell, or otherwise acquire or dispose of, any security, any derivative, any contract of sale of a commodity for future delivery, any option on or any such security, derivative, any contract of sale of a commodity for future delivery, any option on any such security, derivative, or contract, or *any other security or financial instrument that the appropriate … agencies …may, by rule … determine.*"[84]

Some definitions are substantially similar to those in the Senate bill (e.g., "nonbank financial company" and "sponsor"). In addition, there are two new definitions: "trading account" and "illiquid fund." "Trading account" is defined to mean "any account used for acquiring or taking positions in the securities and instruments described [under the definition of "proprietary trading"] … principally for the purpose of selling in the near term (or otherwise with the intent to resell in order to profit from short-term price movements), and any other accounts as the appropriate … agencies … may, by rule … determine." "Illiquid fund" is defined in subsection 619(h)(7) as a hedge fund or private equity fund that "as of May 1, 2010, was principally invested in, or was invested and contractually committed to principally invest in, illiquid assets such as portfolio companies, real estate investments, and venture capital investments; and …[which] makes all investments pursuant to, and consistent with, an investment strategy to principally invest in illiquid assets."

Council Study and Coordinated Joint Rulemaking. Subsection (b) of section 619 requires the Financial Stability Oversight Council to complete a study not later than six months after enactment and make recommendations to the regulators on implementation. The Conference Report, thus, appears to provide the Council less power than the Senate-passed bill, because it limits the Council to recommending how implementation may be geared to (1) promote banking entity safety and soundness; (2) limit inappropriate transfers to "unregulated entities" of the federal subsidies embodied in FDIC deposit insurance and FRS liquidity programs; (3) "protect taxpayers and consumers and enhance financial stability" by minimizing risky activities by banking entities; (4) reduce conflicts of interest between customer interests and the self-interest of the covered entities; (5) limit unduly risky activities of the covered entities; (6) accommodate insurance company investment authority while safeguarding both affiliated banking entities and the financial stability of the United States;[85] and (7) devise appropriate timing for divestiture of illiquid assets affected by implementation of section 619.

Subsection (b) requires the federal banking regulators and the SEC and CFTC to conduct joint rulemaking and to adopt these rules no later than nine months after the Council completes its study. The regulators must coordinate the regulations for safety and soundness and elimination of the possibility of advantaging or disadvantaging some companies. Subsection (c) specifies that final rules are to become effective 12 months after they are issued or two years after enactment. In general, banking entities will be given two years to divest nonconforming activities.

Divestiture of Nonconforming Activities. Subsection (c) addresses divestiture of nonconforming activities. Divestiture of nonconforming activities is generally required within two years of enactment subject to certain exceptions. The FRB is to issue rules on the divestiture provisions within six months of enactment. Additional capital and other restrictions, including margin requirements, on ownership interests in or sponsorship of hedge funds or private equity funds by banking entities are to be implemented by rules promulgated within the context of the joint rulemaking. The two-year divestiture requirement may be extended under certain circumstances: (1) the FRB may approve extensions for one-year periods not to exceed three additional years, and (2) if a contractual obligation in effect on May 1, 2010, requires a banking entity to take or retain its ownership interest in, or provide additional capital to, an illiquid fund, the entity may apply to the FRB for an extension which may be granted for no more than five years; divestiture would be required at the end of the five years or on the contractual date—whichever is earlier.

Permitted Activities. Subsection (d) identifies exceptions to the blanket prohibitions of subsection 619(a) by listing permitted activities and setting conditions under which those activities may be conducted. It excludes from permitted activities any transaction or class of activities, otherwise permitted, that would involve or result in a material conflict of interest; a material exposure by the banking entity to "high-risk assets or high-risk trading strategies" as defined by the regulators; or a threat to safety and soundness of the banking entity or to the financial stability of the United States. It provides standards by which the regulators may set further limits or conditions on these activities and includes authority for the regulators to add to the list of permitted activities. The regulators may impose additional capital and quantitative limits as "appropriate to protect the safety and soundness of banking entities engaged in such activities." Among the conditions specified for conducting these activities are that the activity must (1) be permitted under other federal or state law; (2) be subjected to restrictions as determined by the appropriate federal regulators; and (3) not involve or result in a material conflict of interest, expose the banking entity to "high-risk assets or high-risk trading strategies," or threaten safety and soundness of the banking entity or the financial stability of the United States. Subject to those conditions, the exceptions or permitted activities are:

- **Organizing and Advising Hedge or Private Equity Funds in Connection with Fiduciary or Trust Services**. Subsection (d)(1)(G) authorizes banking entities to organize and offer private equity or hedge funds only if (1) the banking entity provides "bona fide trust, fiduciary, or investment advisory services"; (2) the fund is offered only in connection with trust, fiduciary, or investment advisory services to "persons that are customers of such services of the banking entity"; (3) the banking entity retains only a de minimis interest in the funds;[86] (4) the banking entity and its affiliates engage in no transaction with the fund that would be designated as a covered transaction under FRA section 23A and other transactions with the fund are conducted only on terms specified in FRA section 23B, as if the banking entity were a member bank, and the fund an affiliate of that bank; (5) the banking entity does not guaranty the obligations of the hedge fund or private equity fund; (6) the banking entity does not share a name with the hedge fund or private equity fund; (7) no director or employee of the banking entity, other than a director or employee directly engaged in providing investment advisory or other services to the hedge fund or private equity fund, takes or retains an interest in the fund; and (8) the banking entity takes certain steps to assure the investors in the hedge fund or private equity fund that losses of the fund will be borne solely by its investors.

- **Government and GSE Obligations.** Subsection (d)(1)(A) authorizes the purchase and sale of U.S. obligations; obligations of federal agencies; obligations of Ginnie Mae, Fannie Mae, Federal Home Loan Banks, Farmer Mac, and Farm Credit System institutions; and obligations of any state or political subdivision of a state.
- **Market Making Activities.** Subsection (d)(1)(B) authorizes the "purchase, sale, acquisition, or disposition of securities and various instruments which the regulators have determined by rule to fall within the definition of "proprietary trading" under subsection (h)(4), provided the transactions are "in connection with underwriting or market-making related activities, to the extent that … [such transactions] are designed not to exceed the reasonably expected near term demands of clients, customers, or counterparties."
- **Risk Mitigating Hedging Activities.** Subsection (d)(1)(C) authorizes "risk-mitigating hedging activities" that are related to "positions, contracts, or other holdings of the banking entity and are designed to reduce specific risks in connection with and related to such holdings.
- **Small Business Investment Company Investments.** Subsection (d)(1)(E) authorizes specified small business investment company investments and investments qualified as rehabilitation expenditures with respect to qualified rehabilitated building or certified historic

structure as defined in section 47 of the Internal Revenue Code or similar state historic tax credit program.

- **Insurance Company Portfolio Investments.** Subsection (d)(1)(F) authorizes the "purchase, sale, acquisition, or disposition of securities and other instruments" which the regulators have determined by rule to fall within the definition of "proprietary trading" under subsection (h)(4) if the transactions are "by a regulated insurance company directly engaged in the business of insurance for the general account of the company by any affiliate of such regulated insurance company, provided that such activities by any affiliate are solely for the general account of the regulated insurance company." The transactions must also comply with applicable law, regulation, or guidance, and there must be no determination by the regulators that a relevant law, regulation, or guidance is insufficient to protect the safety and soundness of the banking entity or the financial stability of the United States.
- **Proprietary Trading by Foreign Companies Conducted Outside the United States.** Subsections (d)(1)(H) and (I) authorize investments permitted under sections 4(c)(9) and 4(c)(13) of the Bank Holding Company Act,[87] provided they are conducted solely outside the United States by a company not controlled directly or indirectly by a company organized under the laws of the United States or of a state.
- **Other Investments**. Subsection (d)(1)(J) provides the regulators with authority to permit "[s]uch other activity … by rule, … [as] would promote and protect the safety and soundness of the banking entity and the financial stability of the United States."
- **De Minimis Investments by Banking Entities in Hedge Funds and Private Equity Funds.** Subsection 619(d)(4) permits banking entities, subject to certain limitations, to make and retain a "de minimis investment" in a hedge fund or private equity fund or to make an initial investment in a hedge fund or private equity fund that the banking entity organizes. Among the limitations is a requirement to seek unaffiliated investors to reduce, within one year (subject to a possible extension for two more years), the banking entity's initial investment to the prescribed de minimis amount, as defined in subsection (d)(4). A de minimis investment must be (1) "not more than 3 percent of the total ownership interests of the fund," (2) "immaterial to the banking entity, as defined by rule" and (3) such that the aggregate investment of the banking entity in all such funds

does not exceed 3 percent of its Tier 1 capital. There is also a requirement that a banking entity's aggregate outstanding de minimis or initial investments in hedge funds or private equity funds organized by the banking entity, including retained earnings, must be deducted from assets and tangible equity of the banking entity and the amount of the deduction to "increase commensurate with the leverage of the hedge fund or private equity fund."

Limitation on Relationships with Hedge Funds and Private Equity Funds. Under subsection 619(f), a banking entity serving as "an investment manager, investment advisor, or investment sponsor to a hedge fund or private equity fund" or a banking entity which organizes and offers a hedge fund or private equity fund in connection with fiduciary or trust services as specified in subsection (d)(1)(G) or any affiliates thereof may enter into a transaction with the fund which would be a covered transaction under FRA section 23A if the banking entity and affiliate were a member bank and the fund were an affiliate thereof. In addition, any transaction between the banking entity and the fund must comply with Section 23B of the FRA as if the banking entity were a member bank and the fund, an affiliate, thereof. The FRB may permit a banking entity to enter into a prime brokerage transaction with any hedge fund or private equity fund in which a hedge fund or private equity fund managed, sponsored, or advised by the banking entity or nonbank financial company has an ownership interest under certain conditions. The banking entity must be in compliance with all of the conditions under which a banking entity may organize and advise a hedge fund or private equity fund in connection with fiduciary or trust services under subsection (d)(1)(G). Moreover, the banking entity's chief executive officer must provide an annual, and updated as necessary, written certification of compliance. The FRB must have determined that the primary brokerage agreement is consistent with the safe and sound operation of the banking entity; moreover, the prime brokerage transaction is subject to FRA section 23B as if the counterparty were an affiliate of the banking entity. Additional capital charges or other restrictions for nonbank financial companies are to be covered by rules issued by the appropriate regulators in the prescribed joint rulemaking proceedings.

Anti-Evasion Provision. Subsection (e) authorizes the appropriate regulator, having reasonable cause to believe that a banking entity or a nonbank financial company supervised by the FRB, is engaged in activities functioning as an evasion of section 619, or in violation of section 619, to order, subject to notice and opportunity for a hearing, termination of the activity and disposition of the investment. This subsection also requires the regulators to issue internal control and recordkeeping rules to insure compliance with section 619.

Rules of Construction. Subsection 619(g) provides three rules of statutory construction for interpreting section 619: (1) the prohibitions and restrictions of section 619 apply, except as provided in the section, notwithstanding the existence of other provisions of law authorizing such activities; (2) nothing in section 619 is to "be construed to limit the ability of a banking entity or nonbank financial company … to sell or securitize loans in a manner otherwise permitted by law"; and (3) nothing in section 619 is to "be construed to limit the inherent authority of any Federal agency or State regulatory authority under otherwise applicable provisions of law."

FUTURE PROSPECTS: RULEMAKING AND MANDATED STUDY

While the Conference Committee was at work, there appeared to be some apprehension within the financial services industry about the reach of § 619, the imprecision of its definitions and prohibitions, and its implementation.[88] Some concerns may have been allayed by the Conference Report's final version of section 619. For example, there are specific provisions providing for (1) distinct treatment for insurance company portfolio investments; (2) the ability of banking entities and non-financial companies determined to be systemically important to sponsor hedge fund and private equity funds that are limited to customer investments; (3) conditions under which bank investments in hedge funds and private equity funds may be permitted; and (4) phase-in periods. Although the outlines of a new regulatory framework for proprietary trading and hedge fund operations of banking entities and other systemically important companies are fully outlined in the legislation, the actual reach and practical effect of the provisions await the clarifying hand of the regulators. To illustrate, subsection (d)(1)(C) authorizes banking entities to engage in "risk-mitigating hedging activities" related to "positions, contracts, or other holdings of the banking entity that are designed to reduce specific risks to a banking entity in connection with and related to such positions, contracts or other holdings." It delineates no parameters for these hedging activities. With this and other provisions of the bill, there is likely to be an intensive rulemaking process wherein virtually every possible interpretation of the statutory language will be subjected to a full airing.

It also might be noted that a related provision of the legislation provides clear indication that Congress will continue to monitor the scope of investment activities permitted to banking concerns. Section 620 of the Conference Report gives the federal banking agencies 20 months to study and report on investment and other activities that banking entities may conduct under federal and state law. The agencies are to evaluate and make recommendations on (1) types of activities or investments; (2) associated risks; (3) risk mitigation activities; (4) safety and soundness concerns; (5) potential negative effects of each activity with respect to banking entities and the U.S. financial system; (6) whether each activity or investment is appropriate for banking entities; and (7) any necessary additional restrictions.

APPENDIX A. TEXT OF H.R. 4173 § 1117, AS PASSED BY THE HOUSE

SEC. 1117. RESTRICTION ON PROPRIETARY TRADING BY DESIGNATED FINANCIAL HOLDING COMPANIES.

(a) In General- If the Board determines that propriety trading by a financial holding company subject to stricter standards poses an existing or foreseeable threat to the safety and soundness of such company or to the financial stability of the United States, the Board may prohibit such company from engaging in propriety trading.

(b) Exceptions Permitted- The Board may exempt from the prohibition of subsection (a) proprietary trading that the Board determines to be ancillary to other operations of such company and not to pose a threat to the safety and soundness of such company or to the financial stability of the United States, including—

(1) making a market in securities issued by such company;

(2) hedging or managing risk;

(3) determining the market value of assets of such company; and

(4) propriety trading for such other purposes allowed by the Board by rule.

(c) Rulemaking Authority- The primary financial regulatory agencies of banks and bank holding companies shall jointly issue regulations to carry out this section. (d) Effective Date- The provisions of this section shall take effect after the end of the 180-day period beginning on the date of the enactment of this title. (e) Proprietary Trading Defined- For purposes of this section and with respect to a company, the term 'proprietary trading' means the trading of stocks, bonds, options, commodities, derivatives, or other financial instruments with the company's own money and for the company's own account

(d) Effective Date- The provisions of this section shall take effect after the end of the 180-day period beginning on the date of the enactment of this title.

Appendix B. Text of H.R. 4173 § 619, as Passed by the Senate, and Which Is Included as Part of the Conference-Base Text of H.R. 4173

SEC. 619. RESTRICTIONS ON CAPITAL MARKET ACTIVITY BY BANKS AND BANK HOLDING COMPANIES.

(a) Definitions- In this section—

(1) the terms `hedge fund' and `private equity fund' mean a company or other entity that is exempt from registration as an investment company pursuant to section 3(c)(1) or 3(c)(7) of the Investment Company Act of 1940 (15 U.S.C. 80a-3(c)(1) or 80a-3(c)(7)), or a similar fund, as jointly determined by the appropriate Federal banking agencies;

(2) the term `proprietary trading'—

(A) means purchasing or selling, or otherwise acquiring or disposing of, stocks, bonds, options, commodities, derivatives, or other financial instruments by an insured depository institution, a company that controls, directly or indirectly, an insured depository institution or is treated as a bank holding company for purposes of the Bank Holding Company Act of 1956 (12 U.S.C. 1841 et seq.), and any subsidiary of such institution or company, for the trading book (or such other portfolio as the Federal banking

agencies may determine) of such institution, company, or subsidiary; and

(B) subject to such restrictions as the Federal banking agencies may determine, does not include purchasing or selling, or otherwise acquiring or disposing of, stocks, bonds, options, commodities, derivatives, or other financial instruments on behalf of a customer, as part of market making activities, or otherwise in connection with or in facilitation of customer relationships, including risk-mitigating hedging activities related to such a purchase, sale, acquisition, or disposal; and

(3) the term `sponsoring', when used with respect to a hedge fund or private equity fund, means—

(A) serving as a general partner, managing member, or trustee of the fund;

(B) in any manner selecting or controlling (or having employees, officers, directors, or agents who constitute) a majority of the directors, trustees, or management of the fund; or

(C) sharing with the fund, for corporate, marketing, promotional, or other purposes, the same name or a variation of the same name.

(b) Prohibition on Proprietary Trading-

(1) IN GENERAL- Subject to the recommendations and modifications of the Council under subsection (g), and except as provided in paragraph (2) or (3), the appropriate Federal banking agencies shall, through a rulemaking under subsection (g), jointly prohibit proprietary trading by an insured depository institution, a company that controls, directly or indirectly, an insured depository institution or is treated as a bank holding company for purposes of the Bank Holding Company Act of 1956 (12 U.S.C. 1841 et seq.), and any subsidiary of such institution or company.

(2) EXCEPTED OBLIGATIONS-

(A) IN GENERAL- The prohibition under this subsection shall not apply with respect to an investment that is otherwise authorized by Federal law in—

(i) obligations of the United States or any agency of the United States, including obligations fully guaranteed as to principal and interest by the United States or an agency of the United States;

(ii) obligations, participations, or other instruments of, or issued by, the Government National Mortgage Association, the Federal National Mortgage Association, or the Federal Home Loan Mortgage Corporation, including obligations fully guaranteed as to principal and interest by such entities; and

(iii) obligations of any State or any political subdivision of a State.

(B) CONDITIONS- The appropriate Federal banking agencies may impose conditions on the conduct of investments described in subparagraph (A).

(C) RULE OF CONSTRUCTION- Nothing in subparagraph (A) may be construed to grant any authority to any person that is not otherwise provided in Federal law.

(3) FOREIGN ACTIVITIES- An investment or activity conducted by a company pursuant to paragraph (9) or (13) of section 4(c) of the Bank Holding Company Act of 1956 (12 U.S.C. 1843(c)) solely outside of the United States shall not be subject to the prohibition under paragraph (1), provided that the company is not directly or indirectly controlled by a company that is organized under the laws of the United States or of a State.

(c) Prohibition on Sponsoring and Investing in Hedge Funds and Private Equity Funds-

(1) IN GENERAL- Except as provided in paragraph (2), and subject to the recommendations and modifications of the Council under subsection (g), the appropriate Federal banking agencies shall, through a rulemaking under subsection (g), jointly prohibit an insured depository institution, a company that controls, directly or indirectly, an insured depository institution or is treated as a bank holding company for purposes of the Bank Holding Company Act of 1956 (12 U.S.C. 1841 et seq.), or any subsidiary of such institution or company, from sponsoring or investing in a hedge fund or a private equity fund.

(2) APPLICATION TO FOREIGN ACTIVITIES OF FOREIGN FIRMS- An investment or activity conducted by a company pursuant to paragraph (9) or (13) of section 4(c) of the Bank Holding Company Act of 1956 (12 U.S.C. 1843(c)) solely outside of the United States shall not be subject to the prohibitions and restrictions under paragraph (1), provided that the company is

not directly or indirectly controlled by a company that is organized under the laws of the United States or of a State.

(d) Investments in Small Business Investment Companies and Investments Designed To Promote the Public Welfare-

(1) IN GENERAL- A prohibition imposed by the appropriate Federal banking agencies under subsection (c) shall not apply with respect an investment otherwise authorized under Federal law that is—

(A) an investment in a small business investment company, as that term is defined in section 103 of the Small Business Investment Act of 1958 (15 U.S.C. 662); or

(B) designed primarily to promote the public welfare, as provided in the 11th paragraph of section 5136 of the Revised Statutes (12 U.S.C. 24).

(2) RULE OF CONSTRUCTION- Nothing in paragraph (1) may be construed to grant any authority to any person that is not otherwise provided in Federal law.

(e) Limitations on Relationships With Hedge Funds and Private Equity Funds-

(1) COVERED TRANSACTIONS- An insured depository institution, a company that controls, directly or indirectly, an insured depository institution or is treated as a bank holding company for purposes of the Bank Holding Company Act of 1956 (12 U.S.C. 1841 et seq.), and any subsidiary of such institution or company that serves, directly or indirectly, as the investment manager or investment adviser to a hedge fund or private equity fund may not enter into a covered transaction, as defined in section 23A of the Federal Reserve Act (12 U.S.C. 371c) with such hedge fund or private equity fund.

(2) AFFILIATION- An insured depository institution, a company that controls, directly or indirectly, an insured depository institution or is treated as a bank holding company for purposes of the Bank Holding Company Act of 1956 (12 U.S.C. 1841 et seq.), and any subsidiary of such institution or company that serves, directly or indirectly, as the investment manager or investment adviser to a hedge fund or private equity fund shall be subject to section 23B of the Federal Reserve Act (12 U.S.C. 371c-1) as if such institution, company, or subsidiary were a member bank and such hedge fund or private equity fund were an affiliate.

(f) Capital and Quantitative Limitations for Certain Nonbank Financial Companies-

(1) IN GENERAL- Except as provided in paragraph (2), and subject to the recommendations and modifications of the Council under subsection (g), the Board of Governors shall adopt rules imposing additional capital requirements and specifying additional quantitative limits for nonbank financial companies supervised by the Board of Governors under section 113 that engage in proprietary trading or sponsoring and investing in hedge funds and private equity funds.

(2) EXCEPTIONS- The rules under this subsection shall not apply with respect to the trading of an investment that is otherwise authorized by Federal law—

(A) in obligations of the United States or any agency of the United States, including obligations fully guaranteed as to principal and interest by the United States or an agency of the United States;

(B) in obligations, participations, or other instruments of, or issued by, the Government National Mortgage Association, the Federal National Mortgage Association, or the Federal Home Loan Mortgage Corporation, including obligations fully guaranteed as to principal and interest by such entities;

(C) in obligations of any State or any political subdivision of a State;

(D) in a small business investment company, as that term is defined in section 103 of the Small Business Investment Act of 1958 (15 U.S.C. 662); or

(E) that is designed primarily to promote the public welfare, as provided in the 11th paragraph of section 5136 of the Revised Statutes (12 U.S.C. 24).

(g) Council Study and Rulemaking-

(1) STUDY AND RECOMMENDATIONS- Not later than 6 months after the date of enactment of this Act, the Council—

(A) shall complete a study of the definitions under subsection (a) and the other provisions under subsections (b) through (f), to assess the extent to which the definitions under subsection (a) and the implementation of subsections (a) through (f) would—

(i) *promote and enhance the safety and soundness of depository institutions and the affiliates of depository institutions;*

(ii) *protect taxpayers and enhance financial stability by minimizing the risk that depository institutions and the affiliates of depository institutions will engage in unsafe and unsound activities;*

(iii) *limit the inappropriate transfer of Federal subsidies from institutions that benefit from deposit insurance and liquidity facilities of the Federal Government to unregulated entities;*

(iv) *reduce inappropriate conflicts of interest between the self-interest of depository institutions, affiliates of depository institutions, and financial companies supervised by the Board, and the interests of the customers of such institutions and companies;*

(v) *raise the cost of credit or other financial services, reduce the availability of credit or other financial services, or impose other costs on households and businesses in the United States;*

(vi) *limit activities that have caused undue risk or loss in depository institutions, affiliates of depository institutions, and financial companies supervised by the Board of Governors, or that might reasonably be expected to create undue risk or loss in such institutions, affiliates, and companies; and*

(vii) *appropriately accommodates the business of insurance within an insurance company subject to regulation in accordance with State insurance company investment laws;*

(B) *shall make recommendations regarding the definitions under subsection (a) and the implementation of other provisions under subsections (b) through (f), including any modifications to the definitions, prohibitions, requirements, and limitations contained therein that the Council determines would more effectively implement the purposes of this section; and*

(C) *may make recommendations for prohibiting the conduct of the activities described in subsections (b) and (c) above a specific threshold amount and imposing additional capital requirements on activities conducted below such threshold amount.*

(2) RULEMAKING- Not earlier than the date of completion of the study required under paragraph (1), and not later than 9 months after the date of completion of such study—

(A) the appropriate Federal banking agencies shall jointly issue final regulations implementing subsections (b) through (e), which shall reflect any recommendations or modifications made by the Council pursuant to paragraph (1)(B); and

(B) the Board of Governors shall issue final regulations implementing subsection (f), which shall reflect any recommendations or modifications made by the Council pursuant to paragraph (1)(B).

(h) Transition-

(1) IN GENERAL- The final regulations issued by the appropriate Federal banking agencies and the Board of Governors under subsection (g)(2) shall provide that, effective 2 years after the date on which such final regulations are issued, no insured depository institution, company that controls, directly or indirectly, an insured depository institution, company that is treated as a bank holding company for purposes of the Bank Holding Company Act of 1956 (12 U.S.C. 1841 et seq.), or subsidiary of such institution or company, may retain any investment or relationship prohibited under such regulations.

(2) EXTENSION-

(A) IN GENERAL- The appropriate Federal banking agency for an insured depository institution or a company described in paragraph (1) may, upon the application of any such company, extend the 2-year period under paragraph (1) with respect to such company, if the appropriate Federal banking agency determines that an extension would not be detrimental to the public interest.

(B) TIME PERIOD FOR EXTENSION- An extension granted under subparagraph (A) may not exceed—

(i) 1 year for each determination made by the appropriate Federal banking agency under subparagraph (A); and

(ii) a total of 3 years with respect to any 1 company.

APPENDIX C. THE CONFERENCE REPORT: SECTION 619

SEC. 619. PROHIBITIONS ON PROPRIETARY TRADING AND CERTAIN RELATIONSHIPS WITH HEDGE FUNDS AND PRIVATE EQUITY FUNDS.

The Bank Holding Company Act of 1956 (12 U.S.C. 1841 et seq.) is amended by adding at the end the following:

"SEC. 13. PROHIBITIONS ON PROPRIETARY TRADING AND CERTAIN RELATIONSHIPS WITH HEDGE FUNDS AND PRIVATE EQUITY FUNDS.

"(a) IN GENERAL.—

"(1) PROHIBITION.—Unless otherwise provided in this section, a banking entity shall not—

"(A) engage in proprietary trading; or

"(B) acquire or retain any equity, partnership, or other ownership interest in or sponsor a hedge fund or a private equity fund.

"(2) NONBANK FINANCIAL COMPANIES SUPERVISED BY THE BOARD.—Any nonbank financial company supervised by the Board that engages in proprietary trading or takes or retains any equity, partnership, or other ownership interest in or sponsors a hedge fund or a private equity fund shall be subject, by rule, as provided in subsection (b)(2), to additional capital requirements for and additional quantitative limits with regards to such proprietary trading and taking or retaining any equity, partnership, or other ownership interest in or sponsorship of a hedge fund or a private equity fund, except that permitted activities as described in subsection (d) shall not be subject to the additional capital and additional quantitative limits except as provided in subsection (d)(3), as if the nonbank financial company supervised by the Board were a banking entity.

"(b) STUDY AND RULEMAKING.—

"(1) STUDY.—Not later than 6 months after the date of enactment of this section, the Financial Stability Oversight Council shall study and make recommendations on implementing the provisions of this section so as to—

"(A) promote and enhance the safety and soundness of banking entities;

"(B) protect taxpayers and consumers and enhance financial stability by minimizing the risk that insured depository institutions and the affiliates of insured depository institutions will engage in unsafe and unsound activities;

"(C) limit the inappropriate transfer of Federal subsidies from institutions that benefit from deposit insurance and liquidity facilities of the Federal Government to unregulated entities;

"(D) reduce conflicts of interest between the self-interest of banking entities and nonbank financial companies supervised by the Board, and the interests of the customers of such entities and companies;

"(E) limit activities that have caused undue risk or loss in banking entities and nonbank financial companies supervised by the Board, or that might reasonably be expected to create undue risk or loss in such banking entities and nonbank financial companies supervised by the Board;

"(F) appropriately accommodate the business of insurance within an insurance company, subject to regulation in accordance with the relevant insurance company investment laws, while protecting the safety and soundness of any banking entity with which such insurance company is affiliated and of the United States financial system; and

"(G) appropriately time the divestiture of illiquid assets that are affected by the implementation of the prohibitions under subsection (a).

"(2) RULEMAKING.—

"(A) IN GENERAL.—Unless otherwise provided in this section, not later than 9 months after the completion of the study under paragraph (1), the appropriate Federal banking agencies, the Securities and Exchange Commission, and the Commodity Futures Trading Commission, shall consider the findings of the study under paragraph (1) and adopt rules to carry out this section, as provided in subparagraph (B).

"(B) COORDINATED RULEMAKING.—

"(i) REGULATORY AUTHORITY.—The regulations issued under this paragraph shall be issued by—

"(I) the appropriate Federal banking agencies, jointly, with respect to insured depository institutions;

"(II) the Board, with respect to any company that controls an insured depository institution, or that is treated as a bank holding company for purposes of section 8 of the International Banking Act, any nonbank financial company supervised by the Board, and any subsidiary of any of the foregoing (other than a subsidiary for which an agency described in subclause (I), (III), or (IV) is the primary financial regulatory agency);

"(III) the Commodity Futures Trading Commission, with respect to any entity for which the Commodity Futures Trading Commission is the primary financial regulatory agency, as defined in section 2 of the Dodd-Frank Wall Street Reform and Consumer Protection Act; and

"(IV) the Securities and Exchange Commission, with respect to any entity for which the Securities and Exchange Commission is the primary financial regulatory agency, as defined in section 2 of the Dodd-Frank Wall Street Reform and Consumer Protection Act.

"(ii) COORDINATION, CONSISTENCY, AND COMPARABILITY.—In developing and issuing regulations pursuant to this section, the appropriate Federal banking agencies, the Securities and Exchange

Commission, and the Commodity Futures Trading Commission shall consult and coordinate with each other, as appropriate, for the purposes of assuring, to the extent possible, that such regulations are comparable and provide for consistent application and implementation of the applicable provisions of this section to avoid providing advantages or imposing disadvantages to the companies affected by this subsection and to protect the safety and soundness of banking entities and nonbank financial companies supervised by the Board.

"(iii) COUNCIL ROLE.—The Chairperson of the Financial Stability Oversight Council shall be responsible for coordination of the regulations issued under this section.

"(c) EFFECTIVE DATE.—

"(1) IN GENERAL.—Except as provided in paragraphs (2) and (3), this section shall take effect on the earlier of—

"(A) 12 months after the date of the issuance of final rules under subsection (b); or

"(B) 2 years after the date of enactment of this section.

"(2) CONFORMANCE PERIOD FOR DIVESTITURE.—A banking entity or nonbank financial company supervised by the Board shall bring its activities and investments into compliance with the requirements of this section not later than 2 years after the date on which the requirements become effective pursuant to this section or 2 years after the date on which the entity or company becomes a nonbank financial company supervised by the Board. The Board may, by rule or order, extend this two-year period for not more than one year at a time, if, in the judgment of the Board, such an extension is consistent with the purposes of this section and would not be detrimental to the public interest. The extensions made by the Board under the preceding sentence may not exceed an aggregate of 3 years.

"(3) EXTENDED TRANSITION FOR ILLIQUID FUNDS.—

"(A) APPLICATION.—The Board may, upon the application of a banking entity, extend the period during which the banking entity, to the extent necessary to fulfill a contractual obligation that was in effect on May 1, 2010, may take or retain its equity, partnership, or other ownership interest in, or otherwise provide additional capital to, an illiquid fund.

"(B) TIME LIMIT ON APPROVAL.—The Board may grant 1 extension under subparagraph (A), which may not exceed 5 years.

"(4) DIVESTITURE REQUIRED.—Except as otherwise provided in subsection (d)(1)(G), a banking entity may not engage in any activity prohibited under subsection (a)(1)(B) after the earlier of—

"(A) the date on which the contractual obligation to invest in the illiquid fund terminates; and

"(B) the date on which any extensions granted by the Board under paragraph (3) expire.

"(5) ADDITIONAL CAPITAL DURING TRANSITION PERIOD.—Notwithstanding paragraph (2), on the date on which the rules are issued under subsection (b)(2), the appropriate Federal banking agencies, the Securities and Exchange Commission, and the Commodity Futures Trading Commission shall issue rules, as provided in subsection (b)(2), to impose additional capital requirements, and any other restrictions, as appropriate, on any equity, partnership, or ownership interest in or sponsorship of a hedge fund or private equity fund by a banking entity.

"(6) SPECIAL RULEMAKING.—Not later than 6 months after the date of enactment of this section, the Board shall issues rules to implement paragraphs (2) and (3).

"(d) PERMITTED ACTIVITIES.—

"(1) IN GENERAL.—Notwithstanding the restrictions under subsection (a), to the extent permitted by any other provision of Federal or State law, and subject to the limitations under paragraph (2) and any restrictions or limitations that the appropriate Federal banking agencies, the Securities and Exchange Commission, and the Commodity Futures Trading Commission, may determine, the following activities (in this section referred to as 'permitted activities') are permitted:

"(A) The purchase, sale, acquisition, or disposition of obligations of the United States or any agency thereof, obligations, participations, or other instruments of or issued by the Government National Mortgage Association, the Federal National Mortgage Association, the Federal Home Loan Mortgage Corporation, a Federal Home Loan Bank, the Federal Agricultural Mortgage Corporation, or a Farm Credit System institution chartered under and subject to the provisions of the Farm Credit Act of 1971 (12 U.S.C. 2001 et seq.), and obligations of any State or of any political subdivision thereof.

"(B) The purchase, sale, acquisition, or disposition of securities and other instruments described in subsection (h)(4) in connection with underwriting or market-making-related activities, to the extent that any such activities permitted by this subparagraph are designed not to exceed the reasonably expected near term demands of clients, customers, or counterparties.

"(C) Risk-mitigating hedging activities in connection with and related to individual or aggregated positions, contracts, or other holdings of a banking entity that are designed to reduce the specific risks to the banking entity in connection with and related to such positions, contracts, or other holdings.

"(D) The purchase, sale, acquisition, or disposition of securities and other instruments described in subsection (h)(4) on behalf of customers.

"(E) Investments in one or more small business investment companies, as defined in section 102 of the Small Business Investment Act of 1958 (15 U.S.C. 662), investments designed primarily to promote the public welfare, of the type permitted under paragraph (11) of section 5136 of the Revised Statutes of the United States (12 U.S.C. 24), or investments that are qualified rehabilitation expenditures with respect to a qualified rehabilitated building or certified historic structure, as such terms are defined in section 47 of the Internal Revenue Code of 1986 or a similar State historic tax credit program.

"(F) The purchase, sale, acquisition, or disposition of securities and other instruments described in subsection (h)(4) by a regulated insurance company directly engaged in the business of insurance for the general account of the company and by any affiliate of such regulated insurance company, provided that such activities by any affiliate are solely for the general account of the regulated insurance company, if—

"(i) the purchase, sale, acquisition, or disposition is conducted in compliance with, and subject to, the insurance company investment laws, regulations, and written guidance of the State or jurisdiction in which each such insurance company is domiciled; and

"(ii) the appropriate Federal banking agencies, after consultation with the Financial Stability Oversight Council and the relevant insurance commissioners of the States and territories of the United States, have not jointly determined, after notice and comment, that a particular law, regulation, or written guidance described in clause (i) is insufficient to protect the safety and soundness of the banking entity, or of the financial stability of the United States.

"(G) Organizing and offering a private equity or hedge fund, including serving as a general partner, managing member, or trustee of the fund and in any manner selecting or controlling (or having employees, officers, directors, or agents who constitute) a majority of the directors, trustees, or management of the fund, including any necessary expenses for the foregoing, only if—

"(i) the banking entity provides bona fide trust, fiduciary, or investment advisory services;

"(ii) the fund is organized and offered only in connection with the provision of bona fide trust, fiduciary, or investment advisory services and only to persons that are customers of such services of the banking entity;

"(iii) the banking entity does not acquire or retain an equity interest, partnership interest, or other ownership interest in the funds except for a de minimis investment subject to and in compliance with paragraph (4);

"(iv) the banking entity complies with the restrictions under paragraphs (1) and (2) of subparagraph (f);

"(v) the banking entity does not, directly or indirectly, guarantee, assume, or otherwise insure the obligations or performance of the hedge fund or private equity fund or of any hedge fund or private equity fund in which such hedge fund or private equity fund invests;

"(vi) the banking entity does not share with the hedge fund or private equity fund, for corporate, marketing, promotional, or other purposes, the same name or a variation of the same name;

"(vii) no director or employee of the banking entity takes or retains an equity interest, partnership interest, or other ownership interest in the hedge fund or private equity fund, except for any director or employee of the banking entity who is directly engaged in providing investment advisory or other services to the hedge fund or private equity fund; and

"(viii) the banking entity discloses to prospective and actual investors in the fund, in writing, that any losses in such hedge fund or private equity fund are borne solely by investors in the fund and not by the banking entity, and otherwise complies with any additional rules of the appropriate Federal banking agencies, the Securities and Exchange Commission, or the Commodity Futures Trading Commission, as provided in subsection (b)(2), designed to ensure that losses in such hedge fund or private equity fund are borne solely by investors in the fund and not by the banking entity.

"(H) Proprietary trading conducted by a banking entity pursuant to paragraph (9) or (13) of section 4(c), provided that the trading occurs solely outside of the United States and that the banking entity is not directly or indirectly controlled by a banking entity that is organized under the laws of the United States or of one or more States.

"(I) The acquisition or retention of any equity, partnership, or other ownership interest in, or the sponsorship of, a hedge fund or a private equity fund by a banking entity pursuant to paragraph (9) or (13) of section 4(c) solely outside of the United States, provided that no ownership interest in such hedge fund or private equity fund is offered for sale or sold to a resident of the United States and that the banking entity is not directly or indirectly controlled by a banking entity that is organized under the laws of the United States or of one or more States.

"(J) Such other activity as the appropriate Federal banking agencies, the Securities and Exchange Commission, and the Commodity Futures Trading Commission determine, by rule, as provided in subsection (b)(2), would promote and protect the safety and soundness of the banking entity and the financial stability of the United States.

"(2) LIMITATION ON PERMITTED ACTIVITIES.—

"(A) IN GENERAL.—No transaction, class of transactions, or activity may be deemed a permitted activity under paragraph (1) if the transaction, class of transactions, or activity—

"(i) would involve or result in a material conflict of interest (as such term shall be defined by rule as provided in subsection (b)(2)) between the banking entity and its clients, customers, or counterparties;

"(ii) would result, directly or indirectly, in a material exposure by the banking entity to high-risk assets or high-risk trading strategies (as such terms shall be defined by rule as provided in subsection (b)(2));

"(iii) would pose a threat to the safety and soundness of such banking entity; or

"(iv) would pose a threat to the financial stability of the United States.

"(B) RULEMAKING.—The appropriate Federal banking agencies, the Securities and Exchange Commission, and the Commodity Futures Trading Commission shall issue regulations to implement subparagraph (A), as part of the regulations issued under subsection (b)(2).

"(3) CAPITAL AND QUANTITATIVE LIMITATIONS.—The appropriate Federal banking agencies, the Securities and Exchange Commission, and the Commodity Futures Trading Commission shall, as provided in subsection (b)(2), adopt rules imposing additional capital requirements and quantitative limitations, including diversification requirements, regarding the activities permitted under this section if the appropriate Federal banking agencies, the Securities and Exchange Commission, and the Commodity Futures Trading Commission determine that additional capital and quantitative limitations are appropriate to protect the safety and soundness of banking entities engaged in such activities.

"(4) DE MINIMIS INVESTMENT.—

"(A) IN GENERAL.—A banking entity may make and retain an investment in a hedge fund or private equity fund that the banking entity organizes and offers, subject to the limitations and restrictions in subparagraph (B) for the purposes of—

"(i) establishing the fund and providing the fund with sufficient initial equity for investment to permit the fund to attract unaffiliated investors; or

"(ii) making a de minimis investment.

"(B) LIMITATIONS AND RESTRICTIONS ON INVESTMENTS.—

"(i) REQUIREMENT TO SEEK OTHER INVESTORS.—A banking entity shall actively seek unaffiliated investors to reduce or dilute the investment of the banking entity to the amount permitted under clause (ii).

"(ii) LIMITATIONS ON SIZE OF INVESTMENTS.—Notwithstanding any other provision of law, investments by a banking entity in a hedge fund or private equity fund shall—

"(I) not later than 1 year after the date of establishment of the fund, be reduced through redemption, sale, or dilution to an amount that is not more than 3 percent of the total ownership interests of the fund;

"(II) be immaterial to the banking entity, as defined, by rule, pursuant to subsection (b)(2), but in no case may the aggregate of all of the interests of the banking entity in all such funds exceed 3 percent of the Tier 1 capital of the banking entity.

"(iii) CAPITAL.—For purposes of determining compliance with applicable capital standards under paragraph (3), the aggregate amount of the outstanding investments by a banking entity under this paragraph, including retained earnings, shall be deducted from the assets and tangible equity of the banking entity, and the amount of the deduction shall increase commensurate with the leverage of the hedge fund or private equity fund.

"(C) EXTENSION.—Upon an application by a banking entity, the Board may extend the period of time to meet the requirements under subparagraph (B)(ii)(I) for 2 additional years, if the Board finds that an extension would be consistent with safety and soundness and in the public interest.

"(e) ANTI-EVASION.—

"(1) RULEMAKING.—The appropriate Federal banking agencies, the Securities and Exchange Commission, and the Commodity Futures Trading Commission shall issue regulations, as part of the rulemaking provided for in subsection (b)(2), regarding internal controls and recordkeeping, in order to insure compliance with this section.

"(2) TERMINATION OF ACTIVITIES OR INVESTMENT.—Notwithstanding any other provision of law, whenever an appropriate Federal banking agency, the Securities and Exchange Commission, or the

Commodity Futures Trading Commission, as appropriate, has reasonable cause to believe that a banking entity or nonbank financial company supervised by the Board under the respective agency's jurisdiction has made an investment or engaged in an activity in a manner that functions as an evasion of the requirements of this section (including through an abuse of any permitted activity) or otherwise violates the restrictions under this section, the appropriate Federal banking agency, the Securities and Exchange Commission, or the Commodity Futures Trading Commission, as appropriate, shall order, after due notice and opportunity for hearing, the banking entity or nonbank financial company supervised by the Board to terminate the activity and, as relevant, dispose of the investment. Nothing in this paragraph shall be construed to limit the inherent authority of any Federal agency or State regulatory authority to further restrict any investments or activities under otherwise applicable provisions of law.

"(f) LIMITATIONS ON RELATIONSHIPS WITH HEDGE FUNDS AND PRIVATE EQUITY FUNDS.—

"(1) IN GENERAL.—No banking entity that serves, directly or indirectly, as the investment manager, investment adviser, or sponsor to a hedge fund or private equity fund, or that organizes and offers a hedge fund or private equity fund pursuant to paragraph (d)(1)(G), and no affiliate of such entity, may enter into a transaction with the fund, or with any other hedge fund or private equity fund that is controlled by such fund, that would be a covered transaction, as defined in section 23A of the Federal Reserve Act (12 U.S.C. 371c), with the hedge fund or private equity fund, as if such banking entity and the affiliate thereof were a member bank and the hedge fund or private equity fund were an affiliate thereof.

"(2) TREATMENT AS MEMBER BANK.—A banking entity that serves, directly or indirectly, as the investment manager, investment adviser, or sponsor to a hedge fund or private equity fund, or that organizes and offers a hedge fund or private equity fund pursuant to paragraph (d)(1)(G), shall be subject to section 23B of the Federal Reserve Act (12 U.S.C. 371c–1), as if such banking entity were a member bank and such hedge fund or private equity fund were an affiliate thereof.

"(3) PERMITTED SERVICES.—

"(A) IN GENERAL.—Notwithstanding paragraph (1), the Board may permit a banking entity to enter into any prime brokerage transaction with any hedge fund or private equity fund in which a hedge fund or private equity fund managed, sponsored, or advised by such banking entity has taken an equity, partnership, or other ownership interest, if—

"(i) the banking entity is in compliance with each of the limitations set forth in subsection (d)(1)(G) with regard to a hedge fund or private equity fund organized and offered by such banking entity;

"(ii) the chief executive officer (or equivalent officer) of the banking entity certifies in writing annually (with a duty to update the certification if the information in the certification materially changes) that the conditions specified in subsection (d)(1)(g)(v) are satisfied; and

"(iii) the Board has determined that such transaction is consistent with the safe and sound operation and condition of the banking entity.

"(B) TREATMENT OF PRIME BROKERAGE TRANSACTIONS.—For purposes of subparagraph (A), a prime brokerage transaction described in subparagraph (A) shall be subject to section 23B of the Federal Reserve Act (12 U.S.C. 371c-1) as if the counterparty were an affiliate of the banking entity.

"(4) APPLICATION TO NONBANK FINANCIAL COMPANIES SUPERVISED BY THE BOARD.—The appropriate Federal banking agencies, the Securities and Exchange Commission, and the Commodity Futures Trading Commission shall adopt rules, as provided in subsection (b)(2), imposing additional capital charges or other restrictions for nonbank financial companies supervised by the Board to address the risks to and conflicts of interest of banking entities described in paragraphs (1), (2), and (3) of this subsection.

"(g) RULES OF CONSTRUCTION.—

"(1) LIMITATION ON CONTRARY AUTHORITY.—Except as provided in this section, notwithstanding any other provision of law, the prohibitions and restrictions under this section shall apply to activities of a banking entity or nonbank financial company supervised by the Board, even if such activities are authorized for a banking entity or nonbank financial company supervised by the Board.

"(2) SALE OR SECURITIZATION OF LOANS.—Nothing in this section shall be construed to limit or restrict the ability of a banking entity or nonbank financial company supervised by the Board to sell or securitize loans in a manner otherwise permitted by law.

"(3) AUTHORITY OF FEDERAL AGENCIES AND STATE REGULATORY AUTHORITIES.—Nothing in this section shall be construed to limit the inherent authority of any Federal agency or State regulatory authority under otherwise applicable provisions of law.

"(h) DEFINITIONS.—In this section, the following nitions shall apply:

"(1) BANKING ENTITY.—The term 'banking entity' means any insured depository institution (as defined in section 3 of the Federal Deposit Insurance Act (12 U.S.C. 1813)), any company that controls an insured depository institution, or that is treated as a bank holding company for purposes of section 8 of the International Banking Act of 1978, and any affiliate or subsidiary of any such entity. For purposes of this paragraph, the term 'insured depository institution' does not include an institution that functions solely in a trust or fiduciary capacity, if—

"(A) all or substantially all of the deposits of such institution are in trust funds and are received in a bona fide fiduciary capacity;

"(B) no deposits of such institution which are insured by the Federal Deposit Insurance Corporation are offered or marketed by or through an affiliate of such institution;

"(C) such institution does not accept demand deposits or deposits that the depositor may withdraw by check or similar means for payment to third parties or others or make commercial loans; and

"(D) such institution does not—

"(i) obtain payment or payment related services from any Federal Reserve bank, including any service referred to in section 11A of the Federal Reserve Act (12 U.S.C. 248a); or

"(ii) exercise discount or borrowing privileges pursuant to section 19(b)(7) of the Federal Reserve Act (12 U.S.C. 461(b)(7)).

"(2) HEDGE FUND; PRIVATE EQUITY FUND.—The terms 'hedge fund' and 'private equity fund' mean an issuer that would be an investment company, as defined in the Investment Company Act of 1940 (15 U.S.C. 80a-1 et seq.), but for section 3(c)(1) or 3(c)(7) of that Act, or such similar funds as the appropriate Federal banking agencies, the Securities and Exchange Commission, and the Commodity Futures Trading Commission may, by rule, as provided in subsection (b)(2), determine.

"(3) NONBANK FINANCIAL COMPANY SUPERVISED BY THE BOARD.—The term 'nonbank financial company supervised by the Board' means a nonbank financial company supervised by the Board of Governors, as defined in section 102 of the Financial Stability Act of 2010.

"(4) PROPRIETARY TRADING.—The term 'proprietary trading', when used with respect to a banking entity or nonbank financial company supervised by the Board, means engaging as a principal for the trading account of the banking entity or nonbank financial company supervised by the Board in any transaction to purchase or sell, or otherwise acquire or dispose of, any security, any derivative, any contract of sale of a commodity for future delivery, any option on any such security, derivative, or contract, or any other security or financial instrument that the appropriate Federal banking agencies, the Securities and Exchange Commission, and the Commodity Futures Trading Commission may, by rule as provided in subsection (b)(2), determine.

"(5) SPONSOR.—The term to 'sponsor' a fund means—

"(A) to serve as a general partner, managing member, or trustee of a fund;

"(B) in any manner to select or to control (or to have employees, officers, or directors, or agents who constitute) a majority of the directors, trustees, or management of a fund; or

"(C) to share with a fund, for corporate, marketing, promotional, or other purposes, the same name or a variation of the same name.

"(6) TRADING ACCOUNT.—The term 'trading account' means any account used for acquiring or taking positions in the securities and instruments described in paragraph (4) principally for the purpose of selling in the near term (or otherwise with the intent to resell in order to profit from short-term price movements), and any such other accounts as the appropriate Federal banking agencies, the Securities and Exchange Commission, and the Commodity Futures Trading Commission may, by rule as provided in subsection (b)(2), determine.

"(7) ILLIQUID FUND.—

"(A) IN GENERAL.—The term 'illiquid fund' means a hedge fund or private equity fund that—

"(i) as of May 1, 2010, was principally invested in, or was invested and contractually committed to principally invest in, illiquid assets, such as portfolio companies, real estate investments, and venture capital investments; and

"(ii) makes all investments pursuant to, and consistent with, an investment strategy to principally invest in illiquid assets. In issuing rules regarding this subparagraph, the Board shall take into consideration the terms of investment for the hedge fund or private equity fund, including contractual obligations, the ability of the fund to divest of assets held by the fund, and any other factors that the Board determines are appropriate.

"(B) HEDGE FUND.—For the purposes of this paragraph, the term 'hedge fund' means any fund identified under subsection (h)(2), and does not include a private equity fund, as such term is used in section 203(m) of the Investment Advisers Act of 1940 (15 U.S.C. 80b-

End Notes

[1] 48 Stat. 74, codified at 15 U.S.C. §§ 77a *et seq.*

[2] Technically, the GSA is the same as the Banking Act of 1933; however, the GSA has come to refer to only four sections (§§ 16, 20, 21, and 32) of that piece of legislation, 48 Stat. 162. GSA §§ 20 and 32, which pertained to affiliation restrictions between banks and securities firms, were repealed by the GLBA. Section 16, which delineates the express powers of banks, and § 21, which makes it illegal for any securities company to engage in deposit taking and preserves the authority of commercial banks to engage in the limited securities activities authorized under the GSA § 16, were not repealed by the GLBA and are still good law. For more detailed information on the GSA, see CRS Report R41181, *Permissible Securities Activities of Commercial Banks Under the Glass-Steagall Act (GSA) and the Gramm-Leach-Bliley Act (GLBA)*, by David H. Carpenter and M. Maureen Murphy.

[3] Another important bar to banks' dealing in securities is the BHCA, administered by the Board of Governors of the Federal Reserve System (FRB). Prior to enactment of the GLBA, the BHCA prohibited companies owning or controlling banks (i.e., bank holding companies (BHCs)), from acquiring "ownership or control ... of any company which is not a bank or ... any company the activities of which had been determined by the ... [FRB] to be so closely related to banking as to be a proper incident thereto." 12 U.S.C. § 1843.

[4] The use of the term "bank" to describe both commercial banks and investment banks can be confusing. The term "investment bank" generally is used to describe financial institutions that are primarily involved in the securities business that are not depository institutions because they do not hold federally insured consumer deposits, and therefore are not technically banks. Bear Stearns, before its acquisition by JP Morgan Chase, and Lehman Brothers, before its failure, were examples of investment banks. The term "commercial bank," on the other hand, usually refers depository institutions, generally, or specifically to a depository institution with a bank charter. There are three primary types of federal depository charters: bank, thrift (a.k.a., savings and loan association), and credit union. Thrifts, like banks, offer federally insured consumer deposits, but thrifts, unlike banks, historically have been mission-oriented through a required focus on residential mortgages and related assets. In order to maintain this concentration, thrifts have been subject to limitations on the types of assets in which they can invest. Credit unions engage in activities similar to those of banks and thrifts, but usually on a more limited basis. Credit unions, unlike most banks and thrifts, are owned by their depositors and are tax-exempt. *The Department of the Treasury Blueprint for a Modernized Financial Regulatory Structure*, Dept. of Treasury, pp. 38-39, Mar. 2008, available at *http://ustreas.gov/press/releases* /reports/Blueprint.pdf. This chapter focuses on banks, not other forms of depository institutions.

[5] 70 Stat. 133; 12 U.S.C. §§ 1841-1850.

[6] 12 U.S.C. § 24(Seventh) (stating, in part: "To exercise ... all such incidental powers as shall be necessary to carry on the business of banking; by discounting and negotiating promissory notes, drafts, bills of exchange, and other evidences of debt; by receiving deposits; by buying and selling exchange, coin, and bullion; by loaning money on personal security; and by obtaining, issuing, and circulating notes according to the provisions of title 62 of the Revised Statutes.").

[7] See, e.g., 12 U.S.C. § 1828.

[8] See, e.g., 12 U.S.C. § 1820(d).

[9] 12 U.S.C. § 1831o; 12 U.S.C. § 1818.

[10] The discount window is the Federal Reserve's authority to lend directly to depository institutions and U.S branches of foreign banks, generally where the depository is unable to acquire funding in the private market. Loans made through the discount window must be sufficiently collateralized and are subject to a interest rate above the federal funds rate. 12 U.S.C. § 343. For more information on the discount window, see *Federal Reserve Discount Window*, Federal Reserve System, available at http://www.frbdiscountwindow.org/discountwindowbook.cfm?hdrID=14&dtlID= 43.

[11] See, generally, CRS Report R40783, *Hedge Funds: Legal Status and Proposals for Regulation*, by Kathleen Ann Ruane and Michael V. Seitzinger.

[12] CRS Report RS22581, *Overview of Major Federal Securities Laws*, by Michael V. Seitzinger.

[13] See, David M. Eaton, *The Commercial Banking-Related Activities of Investment Banks and Other Nonbanks*, 44 Emory L. J. 1187 (1995).

[14] However, in emergency situations, there are two possible ways investment banks may secure credit from the Federal Reserve banks. If they are able to offer U.S. government issued or guaranteed obligations as collateral for their own promissory notes and the Federal Reserve bank, in consultation with the FRB, judges that credit is unavailable elsewhere and that failure to secure credit would have an adverse effect on the U.S. economy, advances may be granted to such individuals, partnerships, or corporations. If they lack adequate eligible security for advances, Section 13(3) of the Federal Reserve Act (FRA) provides a mechanism by which a discount may be secured upon the vote of five or more Members of the FRB. 12 U.S.C. § 343. The applicable Board Regulation, 12 C.F.R. § 201.4(d) reads:

> *Emergency credit for others.* In unusual and exigent circumstances and after consultation with the Board of Governors, a Federal Reserve Bank may extend credit to an individual, partnership, or corporation that is not a depository institution if, in the judgment of the Federal Reserve Bank, credit is not available from other sources and failure to obtain such credit would adversely affect the economy. If the collateral used to secure emergency credit consists of assets other than obligations of, or fully guaranteed as to principal and interest by, the United States or an agency thereof, credit must be in the form of a discount and five or more members of the Board of Governors must affirmatively vote to authorize the discount prior to the extension of credit. Emergency credit will be extended at a rate above the highest rate in effect for advances to depository institutions.

[15] BHCs are companies owning or controlling at least one bank.

[16] P.L. 106-102.

[17] CRS Report R41181, *Permissible Securities Activities of Commercial Banks Under the Glass-Steagall Act (GSA) and the Gramm-Leach-Bliley Act (GLBA)*, by David H. Carpenter and M. Maureen Murphy.

[18] Jerry W. Markham, *Banking Regulation: Its History and Future*, 4 N.C. Banking Inst. 221, 240-44 (2000).

[19] Alan E. Sorcher and Satish M. Kini, *Does the Term "Bank Broker-Dealer" Still Have Meaning?*, 6 N.C. Banking Inst. 227, 233-34 (2002). See, also, Charles K. Whitehead, *Reframing Financial Regulation*, 90 B.U. L. Rev. 1, 17-18 (2010).

[20] Securities Industry Assoc. v. Comptroller of the Currency, 577 F.Supp. 252, 255 (D.C. Cir. 1985) (internal citations omitted) (quoting Letter from James E. Smith, Comptroller of the Currency, to G. Duane Vieth (June 10, 1974), reprinted in [1973-78] Fed. Banking L. Rep. (CCH ¶ 96,272)).

[21] 61 Fed. Reg. 68,750-51 (Dec. 30, 1996), citing Citicorp, J.P. Morgan & Co., and Bankers Trust New York Corp., 73 Fed. Res. Bull. 473 (1987), aff'd, Securities Industry Ass'n v. Board of Governors, 839 F.2d 47, 66 (2d Cir.), cert. denied, 486 U.S. 1059 (1988); Chemical New York Corp., Chase Manhattan Corp., Bankers Trust New York Corp., Citicorp,

Manufacturers Hanover Corp., and Security Pacific Corp., 73 Federal Reserve Bulletin 731 (1987); J.P. Morgan & Co., The Chase Manhattan Corp., Bankers Trust New York Corp., Citicorp, and Security Pacific Corp., 75 Federal Reserve Bulletin 192 (1989), aff'd, Securities Industries Ass'n v. Board of Governors, 900 F.2d 360 (D.C. Cir. 1990).

[22] Bd. of Governors for the Federal Reserve System v. Investment Company Institute, 450 U.S. 46 (1981).

[23] Securities Industry Assoc. v. Bd. of Governors for the Federal Reserve System, 468 U.S. 207 (1984).

[24] It includes activities related to extending credit; real estate appraising; check-guaranty services; collection agency services; credit bureau services; asset management; real estate settlement services; operating industrial loan companies and savings associations; management consulting; employee benefits consulting; career counseling; courier services; various limited insurance services; community development activities; money orders; and data processing.

[25] 12 U.S.C. § 1843(k)(1).

[26] 12 U.S.C. § 1843(k)(4).

[27] 12 C.F.R. § 225.28.

[28] 12 U.S.C. §§ 1843(k)(1) – (3). The GLBA established conditions which must be fulfilled before a BHC may become an FHC: all of the company's depository institution subsidiaries must be well managed and well capitalized, and the company must file a notice with the FRB of its intention to become an FHC, certifying that its depository institution subsidiaries meet those capital and management standards. 12 U.S.C. § 1843(l)(1). There is also an additional requirement applicable to any expansion of activities—that all insured depository affiliates have received a satisfactory rating under the most recent Community Reinvestment Act examination. 12 U.S.C. § 1843(l)(2).

[29] 12 U.S.C. § 1843(k)(4)(H).

[30] 12 C.F.R. §§ 225. 170 – 225.177, promulgated in 66 Fed. Reg. 8466, 8484 (January 31, 2001).

[31] 12 C.F.R. § 225.170(f).

[32] 12 C.F.R. § 225.170(a).

[33] 12 C.F.R. § 225.170(b).

[34] The regulation states that "[a] financial holding company may own or control shares, assets and ownership interests pursuant to this subpart only for a period of time to enable the sale or disposition thereof on a reasonable basis consistent with the financial viability of the financial holding company's merchant banking investment." 12 C.F.R. § 225.172(a).

[35] 12 C.F.R. § 225.172(b)(1).

[36] 12 C.F.R.§ 225.170(d).

[37] 12 C.F.R. § 225.170(e)(1). In addition, there are requirements applicable to the books and records and separate management of the portfolio company. 12 C.F.R. §§ 225.170(e)(2) and (3).

[38] Federal Reserve System Bank Holding Company Supervision Manual § 3907.0.2.3.2, available at http://www.federalreserve.gov/boarddocs/supmanual/bhc/bhc.pdf (stating: "'portfolio company' means any company or entity that is directly or indirectly held, owned, or controlled by an FHC that is using the merchant banking authority, and the company or entity is engaged in an activity that is not authorized for the FHC under section 4 of the BHC Act.").

[39] 12 C.F.R. § 225.171(b)(f).

[40] 12 C.F.R. § 225.171.

[41] 12 C.F.R. §§ 225.171(b)(i) and (ii).

[42] 12 C.F.R. § 225.171(b)(e)(2).

[43] 12 C.F.R. § 225.171(b)(e)(1).

[44] 12 CC.F.R. 225.174(a) sets this level at the lesser of 30% of Tier 1 capital of the FHC or 20% of Tier 1 after investments in private equity funds are excluded.

[45] 12 C.F.R. § 225.173(a).

[46] 12 C.F.R. §§ 225.173(a)(2) – (5).

[47] 12 C.F.R. § 225.173(c).

[48] 12 C.F.R. § 225.173(d)(4). "Control" is determined based on such factors as serving in certain capacities in managing the fund; owning or controlling 25% of a class of voting shares of the fund; or selecting or controlling a majority of the directors of the private equity fund. 12 C.F.R. § 225.173(a)(4).

[49] The transactions covered by sections 23A and 23B include extending credit to an affiliate; purchasing or investing in the securities of an affiliate; accepting the affiliate's securities as collateral for any extension of credit; and guaranteeing obligations of the affiliate. 12 U.S.C.§ 371c(b)(7); 12 C.F.R. § 223.3(h).

[50] 12 U.S.C. § 371c-1. The statute requires that such transactions must be "on terms and under circumstances, including credit standards, that ... are at least as favorable to such bank ... as those prevailing at the time for comparable with or involving other nonaffiliated companies, or ... in the absence of comparable transactions, on terms and under circumstances, including credit standards, that in good faith would be offered to, or would apply, to nonaffiliated companies." 12 U.S.C. § 371c-1(a) (1). It applies to all insured banks. 12 U.S.C. § 371c(e).

[51] Sections 23A and 23B cover certain transactions involving a bank and its "affiliates" and define "affiliates" to include both holding company nonbank affiliates and financial subsidiaries of banks. 12 U.S.C. §§ 371c(b) and 371c-1(d)(1). It places an overall limit of 20% of a bank's capital and surplus on the amount of credit a bank may extend to affiliates[51] and a 10% limit on credit to any single affiliate, with exceptions to these percentages for financial subsidiaries of banks. 12 U.S.C. § 371c(e)(3). Under 12 U.S.C. § 24a(a)(1) there is no limit on the interest that a national bank may hold in a financial subsidiary. This applies to state-chartered banks, as well. 12 U.S.C. § 1828(j)(1) (state-chartered, FDIC-insured banks); 12 U.S.C. § 1468(a) (insured savings banks). Section 23A also prohibits banks from purchasing "low quality assets" from an affiliate. 12 U.S.C. § 371c(a)(3). Section 23B also imposes an arms length requirement on securities sales by a bank to an affiliate, including securities sales that are subject to repurchase agreements, and on other types of transactions including payment of money or services to an affiliate; transactions for which the affiliate is paid for its services to the bank; and, any transactions between the bank and a third party in which the affiliate participates or has a financial interest. 12 U.S.C. § 371c-1(a)(2). The statute provides the FRB with broad authority to "exempt transactions or relationships from the requirements of ... [§ 23A] if it finds such exemptions to be in the public interest ...." 12 U.S.C. §§ 371c(f)(2), 371c-1(2)(B). Under § 23B, the FRB also has authority to exclude a BHC subsidiary from the definition of "affiliate," and, therefore, from coverage under the section.

[52] 12 C.F.R. § 225.176(b).

[53] 12 C.F.R. § 225.176(b)(3).

[54] Fed. Reserve Bd., Supervisory Guidance on Equity Investment and Merchant Banking Activities of Financial Holding Companies, and Other Banking Organizations Supervised by the Federal Reserve (June 22, 2000), available at *http://www.federalreserve.gov/boarddocs/SRLetters/2000/sr0009a1.pdf*.

[55] *Id.* at 13. These are described as

> risk management issues [which] may arise when a banking institution or an affiliate lends to or has other business relationships with: ... a portfolio company; ... the general partner or manager of a private equity fund that has also invested in a portfolio company; or ... a private equity-financed company in which the banking institution does not hold a direct or indirect ownership interest but is an investment or portfolio company of a general partner or fund manager with which the banking organization has other investments.

[56] *Id.* at 13.

[57] 12 U.S.C. § 24a (a)(2)(A).

[58] 12 U.S.C. § 1831w. Essentially, the same conditions apply to state banks as are applicable to national banks with respect to controlling a financial subsidiary. State-chartered banks may conduct "activities that are financial in nature" only if the bank and each of its insured depository affiliates are well capitalized after making the capital deductions dictated for national banks under 12 U.S.C. § 24a(c); the bank complies with the financial and operating standards set for the national banks under 12 U.S.C. § 24a(d); and there is compliance with the restrictions on transactions with affiliates found in §§ 23A and 23B of the Federal Reserve Act, 12 U.S.C. §§ 371c and 371c-1.

[59] 12 U.S.C. § 24a(a)(2)(B).

[60] The GLBA prohibition on merchant banking activities by financial subsidiaries of banks was absolute for the first five years after the GLBA's enactment; thereafter, the FRB and the Secretary of the Treasury have the power jointly to issue rules to permit merchant banking. 12 U.S.C. § 1843 note. To date, no such rules have been issued.

[61] The factors include marketplace and technology changes, and competitive considerations. 12 U.S.C. §§ 1843(k)(3) and (3) and 24a(b), as added by P.L. 106-102, § 103 and 121, 113 Stat. 1338, 1343 and 1374.

[62] 12 U.S.C. §§ 2901 *et seq.*

[63] 12 U.S.C. §§ 24a(a)(2) and (3). The statute provides:

> (2) Conditions and requirements. A national bank may control a financial subsidiary, or hold an interest in a financial subsidiary, only if—...
> (B) the activities engaged in by the financial subsidiary as a principal do not include—
> (i) insuring, guaranteeing, or indemnifying against loss, harm, damage, illness, disability, or death (except to the extent permitted under section 302 or 303(c) of the Gramm-Leach-Bliley Act [15 USCS § 6712 or § 6713(c)]) or providing or issuing annuities the income of which is subject to tax treatment under section 72 of the Internal Revenue Code of 1986 [26 USCS § 72];
> (ii) real estate development or real estate investment activities, unless otherwise expressly authorized by law; or
> (iii) any activity permitted in ... [12 USCS § 1843(k)(4)] [expanded activities available to FHCs], except activities described in section ... [12 USCS § 1843(k)(4)(H)] [merchant banking activities] that may be permitted in accordance with ...[12 USCS § 1843 note] ....
> C) the national bank and each depository institution affiliate of the national bank are well capitalized and well managed;
> (D) the aggregate consolidated total assets of all financial subsidiaries of the national bank do not exceed the lesser of—
> (i) 45 percent of the consolidated total assets of the parent bank; or
> (ii) $ 50,000,000,000;
> (E) except as provided in paragraph (4), the national bank meets any applicable rating or other requirement set forth in paragraph (3); and
> (F) the national bank has received the approval of the Comptroller of the Currency for the financial subsidiary to engage in such activities, which approval shall be based solely upon the factors set forth in this section.
> (3) Rating or comparable requirement.
> (A) In general. A national bank meets the requirements of this paragraph if—
> (i) the bank is 1 of the 50 largest insured banks and has not fewer than 1 issue of outstanding eligible debt that is currently rated within the 3 highest investment grade rating categories by a nationally recognized statistical rating organization; or
> (ii) the bank is 1 of the second 50 largest insured banks and meets the criteria set forth in clause (i) or such other criteria as the Secretary of the Treasury and the Board of Governors of the Federal Reserve System may jointly establish by

regulation and determine to be comparable to and consistent with the purposes of the rating required in clause (i).

(B) Consolidated total assets. For purposes of this paragraph, the size of an insured bank shall be determined on the basis of the consolidated total assets of the bank as of the end of each calendar year.

64 12 U.S.C. § 1832w.

65 Statement of Paul A. Volcker Before the Comm. On Banking, Housing, and urban Affairs of the U.S. Senate 1 (February 2. 2010). *http://banking.senate.gov/public/index.cfm* ?FuseAction=Files.View&FileStore_id=ec787c56-dbd2-4498-bbbd-ddd23b58c1c4.

66 *Id.* at 1.

67 *Id.* at 3.

68 The underlying legislation would effectuate a comprehensive realignment of responsibilities of regulating banks and thrifts, bank and financial holding companies, and subsidiaries thereof. For further information, see CRS Report R40975, *Financial Regulatory Reform and the 111th Congress*, coordinated by Baird Webel.

69 H.R. 4173, as passed by the House, § 1117(c).

70 The Conference Base Text is available at the Senate Committee on Banking, Housing and Urban Affairs website, *http://banking.senate.gov/public/_files/ChairmansMarkofHR4173forConference.pdf*.

71 The reference to "companies treated as bank holding companies" may include (1) companies subjected to supervision by the Board of Governors of the Federal Reserve System (FRB) by a Council determination that material distress at the company could pose a threat to financial stability; (2) intermediate holding companies, which section 167(b) of the bill authorizes the FRB to require nonbank financial companies supervised by the FRB to form in order to segregate their financial activities from commercial or other activities not permissible under the Bank Holding Company Act (BHCA); and (3) supervised securities holding companies, supervised by the FRB and subjected to the requirements of the BHCA under section 618(e)(2) of the bill.

72 The other members are the Chairman of the Board of Governors of the Federal Reserve System, the Comptroller of the Currency, the Chairman of the Securities and Exchange Commission, the Chairperson of the Federal Deposit Insurance Corporation, the Chairperson of the Commodities Futures Trading Corporation, the Director of the Federal Housing Finance Agency, the Director of the Bureau of Consumer Financial Protection (to be established under this legislation), and a presidentially appointed independent member with expertise in the insurance industry.

73 The assignment of authority between the Council and the banking regulators is in some sense novel in terms of current law. This arrangement, coupled with the lack of specific language delineating standards by which the regulators would be able to alter or disregard recommendations of the Council may, however the regulators deal with Council recommendations, result in litigation yielding consequences unforeseen by the drafters of section 619.

74 Under 12 U.S.C. § 24(Eleventh), the conditions under which national banks are permitted to "make investments designed primarily to promote the public welfare" are specified.

75 12 U.S.C. §§ 1843(c)(3) and 1843(c)(9).

76 Transactions covered in § 23A of the Federal Reserve Act, 12 U.S.C. § 371c, are prohibited; transactions covered in § 23 B, 12 U.S.C. § 371c-1, must be on market terms.

77 Section 113 provides for subjecting companies to FRB supervision by a Council determination that material distress at the company could pose a threat to financial stability.

78 Among the factors that the Council is to examine are the extent that the limitations would impact safety and soundness of the covered institutions and companies; protect taxpayers and minimize the risk of unsafe and unsound practices; limit inappropriate transfer to unregulated entities of the federal subsidy provided by deposit insurance and federal liquidity facilities; reduce inappropriate conflicts of interest between the self-interest of the

covered companies and the interests of their customers; impose costs on U.S. households and businesses; limit risky activities in covered companies; and "appropriately accommodate the business of insurance within an insurance company in accordance with State insurance company investment laws."

[79] See, e.g., 12 U.S.C. § 371c(f)(2) (authorizing the FRB "at its discretion, by regulation or order [to] exempt transactions or relationships from the requirements of [§ 23A of the Federal Reserve Act] ... if it finds such exemptions to be in the public interest and consistent with the purposes of this section") and 12 U.S.C. § 371c-1(e)(2)(A) (authorizing the FRB to "exempt transactions or relationships from the requirements of" § 23B of the Federal Reserve Act). FRA §§ 23A and 23B deal with restrictions on interaffiliate transactions within bank holding companies (BHCs). Under § 23B, the FRB also has authority to exclude a BHC subsidiary from the definition of "affiliate," and, therefore, from coverage under the section.

[80] Sections 619(b)(1) (prohibition on proprietary trading); (c)(1) (prohibition on sponsoring and investing in hedge funds and private equity funds); and (f)(1)(capital and quantitative limitations for certain nonbank financial companies).

[81] The Committee Report states:

> The incentive for firms to engage in these activities is clear: when things go well, high-risk behavior can produce high returns....When losses from high-risk activities are significant, they can threaten the safety and soundness of individual firms and contribute to overall financial instability. Moreover, when the losses accrue to insured depositories or their holding companies, they can cause taxpayer losses. In addition, when banks engage in these activities for their own accounts, there is an increased likelihood that they will find that their interests conflict with those of their customers.
>
> The Council recommendations and modifications will be included in a study to assess the extent to which the prohibitions, limitations and requirements of section 619 will promote several goals, including: the safety and soundness of depositories and their affiliates; protecting taxpayers from loss; limiting the inappropriate transfer of economic subsidies from institutions that benefit from deposit insurance and liquidity facilities of the Federal government to unregulated entities; reducing inappropriate conflicts of interest between depositories and their affiliates, or financial companies supervised by the Board of Governors, and their customers; affecting the cost of credit or other financial services, limiting undue risk or loss in financial institutions; and appropriately accommodating the business of insurance within insurance companies subject to State insurance company investment laws.
>
> The Council study is included to assure that the prohibitions included in section 619 work effectively. It is not the intent of the section to interfere inadvertently with longstanding, traditional banking activities that do not produce high levels of risk or significant conflicts of interest. For that reason the Council is given some latitude to make needed modifications to definitions and provisions in order to prevent undesired outcomes. However, it is intended that the Council will determine how to effectively implement the prohibitions and restrictions of the section, and not to weaken them.

S.Rept. 111-___, 111th Cong., 2d Sess. 7 and 74 (2010) to accompany S. 3217, April 30, 2010, available on the website of the Senate Committee on Banking, Housing, and Urban Affairs at http://banking.senate.gov/public/_files/ Comittee_Report_S_Rept_111_176.pdf.

[82] Excluded from the definition of "banking entity" are institutions functioning solely in a trust capacity under specified conditions: substantially all the deposits must be in trust funds; none of its insured deposits are marketed through an affiliate; no demand deposits are accepted or commercial loans made; and the institution does not accepts payment, discount, or borrowing services from the Federal Reserve banks.

[83] Emphasis supplied.

[84] Emphasis supplied.

[85] The actual language reads: "appropriately accommodate the business of insurance within an insurance company subject to regulation in accordance with the relevant insurance company investment laws, while protecting the safety and soundness of any banking entity with which such insurance company is affiliated and of the United States financial system."

[86] A de minimis investment, as defined in subsection (d)(4), is "not more than 3 percent of the total ownership interests of the fund," and "immaterial to the banking entity, as defined by rule" but such that the aggregate investment of the banking entity in all such funds does not exceed 3 percent of its Tier 1 capital.

[87] 12 U.S.C. §§ 1843(c)(3) and 1843(c)(9).

[88] Eric Dash and Nelson D. Swartz, "Bank Lobbyists Make a Final Run at Reform Bill," N.Y. Times (June 20, 2010), available at http://www.nytimes.com/2010/06/21/business/21volcker.html?scp=1&sq=volcker%20rule &st=cse; S.Rept. 111-___, 111th Cong., 2d Sess. 7 and 74 (2010) to accompany S. 3217, April 30, 2010, available on the website of the Senate Committee on Banking, Housing, and Urban Affairs at http://banking.senate.gov/public/_files/Comittee_Report_S_Rept_111_176.pdf

Chapter Sources

The following chapters have been previously published:

Chapter 1 – This is an edited, excerpted and augmented edition of a United States Congressional Research Service publication, Report Order Code R41181, dated April 12, 2010.

Chapter 2 – This is an edited, excerpted and augmented edition of a United States Congressional Research Service publication, Report Order Code R41298, dated June 30, 2010.

INDEX

J

L

M

N

O

P

Q

R